CHOOSING LOVERS
Making better choices for your love life

By

Donald L. Boone

ACKNOWLEDGMENTS

Thanks to those who gave me answers to very personal questions. Sometimes directly, sometimes indirectly. To some it was embarrassing in the beginning conversations, but to the point. They shall remain nameless here, and they may be surprised to learn they were not the only ones to feel or to be this way.

Thanks to my life's mate who lets me play in the field of writing, though who sometimes questions my field of interests. Understandably.

TABLE OF CONTENTS

INTRODUCTION. 10

THE PROBLEMS WITH VENUS. .13
Aries
  Venus 17
Taurus
  Venus 20
Gemini
  Venus 21
Cancer
  Venus 22
Leo
  Venus 24
Virgo
  Venus 25
Libra
  Venus 27
Scorpio
  Venus 29
Sagittarius
  Venus 31
Capricorn
  Venus 32
Aquarius
  Venus 34
Pisces
  Venus 35

PERSONAL TIPS	.36
THE POINT of SELF	.39
VIRGINITY LOST	.41
Chart 1A	.43, 109
Chart 2A	.46 111
Chart 3A	.48
Chart 4A	.50
Chart 5A	.52
Chart 6A	.54
PROBLEM PLANETS IN HOUSES	.56
Venus in the first	.57
Venus in Aries	.59
Venus in Scorpio	.59
Venus in Capricorn	.60
Venus in Aquarius	.60
Venus in the third	.61
Venus in the twelfth	.62
Venus in the fifth.	.63
Venus in the second	.66
Venus in the fourth	.68
Venus in the sixth	.69
Venus in the seventh	.71
Venus in the eighth	.73
Venus in the ninth	.74
Venus in the tenth	.76
Venus in the eleventh	.77

PROBLEM PLANETS
IN THE SEVENTH HOUSE
- Sun 79
- Moon 80
- Mercury 81
- Venus 82
- Mars 83
- Jupiter 84
- Saturn 85
- Uranus 86
- Neptune 87
- Pluto 88

PROBLEM LOVERS OF THE SIXTH. .89
and TWELFTH HOUSE

SEXUAL GENDER INFLUENCES OF THE
SUN SIGNS 93

SEXUAL INTERESTS OF THE
SUN SIGNS 95

SPECIAL NOTES 100

SEXUAL HOUSES 101
- Second house 102
- Fifth house 102
- Eighth house 103
- Eleventh house 103

PLANETARY ASPECTS . . .104

ASPECTS of INTEREST . . .113

QUARTER COMPOSITES & THE
INDIVIDUAL CONCERNED . .118
    First Quarter 120
    Second Quarter . . .122
    Third Quarter . . .123
    Fourth Quarter . . .124

THE LIGHT AND DARK PARTS
OF A CHART 126

THE CYCLES OF MARRIAGE
AND DIVORCE 129
  Marriage 131
  Divorce 132
  Turning the corner . . .134
  Mid life crisis 135
  The last chance 137
  Looking again 137

YOUR MARITAL BLISS, OR IS IT? .138
    Cancer 140
    Taurus 141
    Capricorn 142
    Scorpio 143
    Virgo 144
    Aquarius 145
    Leo 146
    Pisces 147
    Libra 148
    Gemini 149
    Aries 151
    Sagittarius 152

SUN, MOON, AND ASCENDING SIGN
COMBINATIONS 153
STELLIUMS 154
THE YEARS WE STRUGGLE. . .157
   First 158
   Second 161
   Third 163

THE SEXUAL OUTLOOK . . .164
   Aries male 165
   Aries Female 167
   Taurus Male 169
   Taurus Female 170
   Gemini Male 172
   Gemini Female 173
   Cancer Male 175
   Cancer Female 176
   Leo Male 178
   Leo Female 180
   Virgo Male 182
   Virgo Female 184
   Libra Male 186
   Libra Female 187
   Scorpio Male 189
   Scorpio Female 191
   Sagittarius Male 192
   Sagittarius Female . . .194
   Capricorn Male 195
   Capricorn Female . . .196
   Aquarius Male 197
   Aquarius Female 199
   Pisces Male 201
   Pisces Female 202

FINDING YOUR MATE	.204
Fire & Fire	.207
Earth & Earth	.211
Air & Air	.215
Water & Water	.220
WOMEN SEEKING MEN	.224
Aries	.225
Taurus	.226
Gemini	.227
Cancer	.228
Leo	.229
Virgo	.230
Libra	.231
Scorpio	.232
Sagittarius	.233
Capricorn	.234
Aquarius	.235
Pisces	.236
MEN SEEKING WOMEN	.237
Aries	.238
Taurus	.239
Gemini	.241
Cancer	.243
Leo	.245
Virgo	.246
Libra	.247
Scorpio	.248
Sagittarius	.249
Capricorn	.251
Aquarius	.253
Pisces	.255

TRANSSEXUALS	.256
EMOTIONAL CYCLES	.261
Charts	.263
NIGHT OR DAY PERSON	.267
SIGNS and SYMBOLS	.268
GLOSSARY	.269

INTRODUCTION

As someone who understands the impact of Venus in Capricorn in the first house, I thought others should know about this part of life. Sexual addiction is the reason why this book found its way into your hands. The addiction to sex is very real and it creates continuous problems for those who are addicted. It also causes problems for those who live with them. Especially if they are not well matched in needs. When you form new relationships you must make the best decision you can based on your personal knowledge at the time. Something you must be aware of is, is the relationship to be formed for marital reasons, or just for the fun and games. Many of us are in relationships that leave us frustrated, and there are those who are fortunate in their relationships. Most of us are at a loss to explain why we are the way we are personally. Perhaps the information found here will make your love life easier to understand.

When you become a student of Astrology, you will come to understand that Venus, the planet of love, may be the planet that causes the greatest amount of problems in your life. Other planets can be the cause of natural conditions coming into play in your life. Perhaps they caused the original ignition of the sexual flames. Either way, once the sexual fires are started they may not be easily extinguished for years to come. It is important as to how you were introduced to your sexual nature. Was it good, or bad?

In the long run it is Venus that is responsible for the pleasures you seek, whatever they may be, and Venus will control the directions you travel seeking fulfillment. You may attempt to control the events caused by Venus, yet Venus will control your way of thinking. Venus is the planet that brings enjoyments into our lives, no matter what, or how, those joys are used to fulfill your needs. What is enjoyable to one person, can be distasteful to another.

The major problem caused by the planet Venus, is in choosing the wrong mate in life. Especially when the person you choose does not have the same sexual needs as yourself. The knowledge offered in this book will put you in a better position to understand what you are letting yourself in for with most planetary combinations. This book may help you decide which Sun sign is best for you, and which planetary positions best suit your lifestyle. You shouldn't choose beyond your personal capabilities.

When you consider that 33% of the Astrological Sun signs suffer with an addiction of some kind; they in turn affect another 33% through their association as mates or lovers. In the long term everyone is affected in some manner by those who are addicted. The question is, Which part of the percentage do you fall into and how do you want to control your involvement.

You, as the reader, need to understand that this book, and the events it brings to light, is not written to judge the events or the life styles of the people that are described herein. Life happens.

As you look at the various charts used in this book, remember they are here for demonstrations only. They will not contain the time, date, and place of birth. They will not include the planetary degrees and minutes. These charts are used only to help inform you in seeking the same kind of information in your own charts, or those of others.

PROBLEMS CAUSED BY VENUS

You must remember that the information presented here is concerned only with an individual's love life and is general in nature. To delineate and better understand the actual events caused by the presence of Venus in any location in your life, or any of the other planets discussed here, and what conditions they produce in any one individual's life, would require a correct Natal chart done on that individual. Do not confuse this information with a person's Sun sign because it is a vastly different area. A correct Natal chart requires the time, date, and place of birth. Anything less is incorrect.

At times, where the Constellation Venus is found at birth can be a godsend to some, or a curse to others. The difference between the two has to be determined by the person in whose chart the condition has an influence. Even then the effects can be good or bad depending on a person's life at the time of any particular event. Each of the twelve Sun signs of the zodiac are no doubt different and so are their requirements for personal love.

To the person who has any of these Venus placements the influence will, of course, seem natural, which it is in their life. They often find it strange that someone else can be so different from themselves. Consider a woman who has Venus in Virgo and she is acquainted with a woman who has Venus in Scorpio. The woman with Venus in Virgo may seem nearly celibate to the woman with Venus in Scorpio. The woman with Venus in Scorpio will think of the woman with Venus in Virgo as an ice cube or as a frigid bitch. The woman with Venus in Virgo has an understanding of her own sexual needs, yet in her mind she may refer to the woman with Venus in Scorpio, as a whore. Both are comfortable with their own personal sexual nature. The problem they both have is in understanding how the other person's sexual makeup seems to be so natural for them when it is so radically different from their own nature.

An easier way to understand the differences of the Venus influence in your life is to understand the strengths or weaknesses of each Venus position. As an example, someone with Venus in Cancer or Taurus, may be very fond of food. Ask a person who has trouble keeping their weight down, what they think about most of the time. It is, of course, food they think about. Ask someone who has a strong Venus in Aries, Scorpio, Capricorn, or Aquarius what they think about most of the time. More often than not it starts the moment they wake up in the morning, and the first thought can easily be about going to bed with someone of the opposite sex. Especially if Venus is found in the first house, as this is the house of our physical nature. If you choose your mate incorrectly you might find cookie crumbs in your bed instead of the lover you desire.

When you become truly aware of people, it is very common to develop an ability to sense someone's aura, or their personal space. This personal space is often involved in the attracting or diverting of the opposite sex. A person with a close and tight aura, will not easily let others inside. Yet, someone with a large aura, often emanating from a confident and wanting person, may attract prospective mates like bees to honey, or Humming birds to containers of sugar water.

When you find Venus in the signs of Aries, Capricorn, Scorpio, or Aquarius, this may be someone who considers every person of the opposite sex as a potential sex partner. Most of those they consider originally, are quickly discarded from the mind. A few are considered a little longer and on occasion, one or two are never discarded. Those not discarded from the mind are held in a secret mental file in the back of the mind. This is just in case they are needed later for a potential sexual mating.

Also, the influences of Venus can be directed in a variety of ways. Altering where, and how, the love is used. An example of this can be seen in the elderly. These are often people who no longer have a mate with which to share their life and love. These folks can be found doting on a small animal, or a house and yard full of plants.

Of course, Venus in these positions occur at different times of the year, and the influences are imprinted on the individual's character at the time of birth. Consequently, we will start at the beginning of the Astrological signs for Venus and progress through them together.

VENUS IN ARIES

Sexual indulgence for this person is more a matter of sudden impulse, rather than that of deliberately seeking a lover or a life long mate.

The problem with Venus in this sign is a continual sexual unrest, a hungry void that needs to be filled. Relationships created by a Venus in Aries are, as a rule, unplanned. They just seem to happen. The romantic situations this person finds themselves in often start quickly, and they may end just as quickly. It's as if someone with Venus in Aries never quite gets the chance to enjoy the fruits of their love life. Just ask someone who has a Venus in Aries how their sex life is and most of the time they'll tell you, "It's great." Then ask how their love life is, and they may say, "It stinks." The partner sharing their bed will provide an entirely different answer.

When you encounter someone with a Venus in Aries don't be surprised to have this person make the first verbal communication, perhaps even the first physical body touch, male or female. However, if you are someone they have chosen as a lover, and if you take too long making up your mind about accepting their offer, they may have moved on to someone else. Someone who does not hesitate in responding.

The person with Venus in Aries often tends to seek someone of a weaker nature. However, this may not take place on a conscious level. The male often seems attracted to the beauty, and apparent helplessness, of some women. Women who have Venus in this constellation, may be a bit too masterful and too self-confident for most men to handle. Because of this condition, a woman with Venus in Aries may have problems finding a mate who is strong enough for the style of her love life, or her lifetime requirements.

If you are someone with Venus in Aries, and you choose the wrong partner to share your life, it can result in a sexual weakness in the male and a sexual indifference in the woman. It can also lead to promiscuous love affairs outside of the relationship, male or female . Jealousy can also be a problem for those with Venus in this constellation.

If you were born with Venus in Aries, you may need to slow down on your sexual quests; you can't make love to all of them, though you may try. The hard part of dealing with Venus in Aries is the seeming inability to stop jumping into bed with someone as soon, or shortly after, meeting them.

For those with Venus in Aries, time seems of importance. They don't want to waste any as they have other things to do. This is someone who will start a love affair now and pay for it later if it becomes boring. Venus in this sign will produce a craving for something. This is one of the four most important signs of the Zodiac and those that can create an addiction. The house it is in will determine how that addiction is fulfilled.

VENUS IN TAURUS

The strength of Venus in Taurus can produce a strong sexual nature. It can also lead to excesses in many other directions, especially if it is left unfulfilled. The power of Venus in this sign can lead to the accumulation of things that a person may think they need. Yet, either the male or female can become a steadfast stay-at-home type when they are sexually satisfied, or if they are very happy and contented in their personal surroundings. As it happens they can be lead through life by their mates, often in a desired direction, with affection.

This Sun sign has a tendency to look at their mates, and their families, as possessions, because this is a Sun sign that accumulates things. However, this same condition of possessiveness can lead to problems. Especially if their mate is someone who resists being emotionally possessed. Quite often, someone with a strong Venus in Taurus is overly protective of their mates and of their children; even to the point of unknowingly stunting some areas of their personal growth.

This is a very faithful lover when all is well in their home life, and someone with Venus in this sign loves sex when the right relationship has been formed. As a lover, if you've been chosen by this person as their mate, you had better be able to satisfy their sexual needs or move over for someone who can.

VENUS IN GEMINI

It may seem that sex is of a secondary interest to someone with Venus in Gemini. In general, the men are stimulated by the visual experience, and the women enjoy the written or spoken word. This can be a key factor with Venus in Gemini. Men and women with Venus in this sign, can be stimulated to a sexually responsive nature through communications, whether visual or written. For the woman, sometimes a single favorite flower, and a note from her lover confessing his feelings, may be all that is needed to kindle her fires.

A person born with Venus in this constellation can appear to others as cold, or lacking in affection and, perhaps, even lacking some moral judgment. This can be a person who likes to experiment sexually or who is subject to sexual perversion, though sexual perversion differs from mind to mind. What perversion is to one person may be perfectly normal to another.

Venus in Gemini can be a person who is in a romantic mood one minute, and out of the mood the next. The position of Venus in a dual sign such as Gemini, can bring about bigamist situations as well. Remember, as a dual sign, Gemini may enjoy more than one partner simultaneously. The problem is in their not knowing if they have made the right choice. Of course, for them, this question comes up with every lover, whether it is the same sex or not.

VENUS IN CANCER

This is the romantic individual, and they have a healthy craving for love. Part of the problem is in finding a suitable mate early in their life. Too often, it seems they have to search until their later years to find the love life they have been searching for all of their lives. Even then, they may just settle for someone they are with at the time they call off the continual search.

However, this is one of the more faithful marital mates in the Zodiac, and it is one of the more emotional signs. It takes a strong individual to stand the roller coaster ups and downs of this emotional mind. Take care not to criticize, or to ridicule this individual's love making. If you do, they will be gone like a shot as they can easily leave a loved one pondering what happened. If they should stick around after you criticize them, you'll have a very deeply affected relationship. Communication and understandings with this partner are a very important part of the relationship.

A person with Venus in Cancer may not be able to tell you verbally about their emotional needs, as they cannot express their feelings to others easily. Because of this condition, frustrations in their love life can lead to upsetting conditions in their mind.

This mental condition can produce a lover who nags their mate and, often, not in a subtle manner.

If, as an outsider, you ask them a question about their love life, watch them sidestep the issue when there is a problem at home, or in their bedroom. This is someone who will answer a question with a question.

VENUS IN LEO

As a lover, someone born with Venus in Leo will often become a strong protector of their chosen mate. The male does like to be looked up to and admired by women. This is often the man referred to as the 'Lady killer.' A man who is likely considered, handsome.

The Leo woman will be the perfect host, but she is not shy in seeking admiration from whomever will bestow it. As her mate in life you will be expected to put jewelry on her fingers, simply because she likes to display her wealth, and as a male, your wealth is hers.

It is not certain who actually suffers from the problems of having Venus in Leo; the individual with Venus in Leo or the lover. This is a show and tell person, and it can be costly to maintain the limelight they seek. Will it be nice homes, nice cars, jewelry, or simply nudity. Yes nudity. You see, most of the better-known models are of the Sun sign of Leo, and if Venus is in Leo as well, he or she, will be seen somehow.

Often a person with Venus in Leo, will become involved in love affairs that seem to last indefinitely, perhaps continuing even after marriage to another person has taken place. The Leo lover enjoys a picnic under a tree in the meadow, a glass of something to sip on, and making love out of doors.

VENUS IN VIRGO

This can easily become a celibate person. Possibly because they are too busy enjoying the pursuit of knowledge. This can also be a very critical person when it comes to their love life. It is very important for any potential mate interested in this person, to understand their needs before long-term commitments are made. Things that excite some lovers, can easily do just the opposite for the Venus in Virgo position.

Perhaps they require too much perfection in their love life, although they themselves may not realize what it is they are seeking for a total fulfillment in their lives. This person may not like being touched, and at times, they can be repulsed by this seemingly natural event taking place among others. Strange as it seems, Venus in Virgo can produce some unusual sexual relationships in a person's life. Like showering together with a lover, and perhaps even going to bed without drying off with a towel, their bodies still dripping wet. Marriage, when it happens, can bring out a very affectionate mate. This person is faithful to their mates, though sometimes they may seem dull to someone with a higher sexed Venus position.

Venus in this sign often produces someone who is a neatness freak, male or female. And, surprisingly, someone who will strive to be the perfect lover depending on their other natal planets. When you decide you want to spend time with this person, especially the first time, be sure you're clean and wearing clean clothing. Don't be blunt in your speech or crude in your conversation. If you don't heed this information, most likely it will also be your last time spent with this person.

So, is Venus in Virgo a problem? It may not seem so to someone who has this Venus position, but it will definitely seem to be a problem for the other sign positions of Venus. Like those who have Venus in Aries, Capricorn, Aquarius, or Scorpio.

VENUS IN LIBRA

At times it may seem as if the women with this Venus position have little interest in men, but they do seek the male who provides sympathy, love, understanding, and companionship. A person who has Venus in Libra, may be in love with 'love,' and not the realities of life.

Because Libra tends to lean toward indecisiveness, the inability to make up one's mind can be a problem for them in most things in life. They spend so much time seeking the correct mate, that it would be a daunting task to most of us.

Can this be a curse? It can be if you are the person who cannot make up their mind, or the person waiting for the decision. Yet, in the end, the time they spent waiting for the right mate serves them well. They wait to find a mate who will offer a pleasant love life, as this Venus in Libra lover will do nearly anything to avoid an unpleasant love situation in their life.

These lovers have a natural charm about them, though even they are often unaware of this part of their personal makeup. The natural charm and grace they possess will draw others to them as if by magnetism.

Neither the male, nor female, may seem to have a great need for sex, though they sometimes may appear too. Yet, both male and female will crave admiration and flattery from others. This Venus lover enjoys dressing in sexually stimulating attire, whether it's a formal dress occasion or a nearly naked event.

VENUS IN SCORPIO

To be born with Venus in Scorpio, is to be cursed with a hearty sexual appetite if it is in the first house of physical being. If you are seeking a mate, take care in choosing a lover with this Venus position. If you make the wrong choice, you may not be up to the continual excessive love play, as this is a strong and intense lover. This person makes love with their whole being, and if you cannot keep up with their needs, prepare to be devoured. The male or female may encounter or suffer from intense jealousy, especially if you are not taking care of their needs.

Venus, in this sign, will bring with it a craving for something. This is one of the four most important signs of the Zodiac that can create an addiction. The house it is in, will determine how that addiction will try to become fulfilled.

The female often gains social position and standing just from the drive and energy produced by this Venus position. This is not a sugar and honey woman, this is a woman of strength and cunning, and if you can't keep up with her, get out of the way.

If the home love life does not serve the male's needs and leaves him unfulfilled, he may seek affection or adventure away from home. If he has sexual contacts outside the home, he will not allow his personal entanglements to affect his domestic life.

Any love affairs outside of the marriage or other unions, are normally kept under careful control, and may never be known about by others.

For either the male or female, the sexual drive is indeed a curse to be reckoned with. It is a hunger, which can drive them continually. Sex is nearly always present in their mind, and somehow, but a short distance from fulfillment.

VENUS IN SAGITTARIUS

This is a lover who cares about what people say or think about them and their love life. Because of this mental circumstance, they will not deviate very far from the established customs of sexual behavior. If they do stray from the marital bed, others may never know it. Promiscuity with this person as a lover, may not produce a long term relationship. For sex without the personal and intimate involvement, is not to their liking.

Should you become involved in an extramarital affair with someone having this Venus position, do not expect public affection. Especially where anyone they know personally may happen to come across the two of you. Even with this kind of thinking, this can be someone with a very flirtatious nature. Someone with Venus in Sagittarius can get caught up in their own flirtatious initiatives, and then a love affair may start that had not been intended. It's as if they get caught up in the excitement of a sporting event.

There can be an inner fire found in this lover, a fire that is very appealing to the opposite sex. To get caught in this flame is to seek it again. If you are someone to have sampled this lover, believe me, you will want to explore that flame again. Take care you don't get burned.

VENUS IN CAPRICORN

This is another Venus position with a strong sexual nature, more so with a first house Venus position. This is an ongoing lustfulness, a lover who will make love with anyone of their choosing. Often someone with Venus in Capricorn just wants to have more than one lover for a variety of lovemaking. Venus, in this sign, will bring with it a craving for something. This is one of the four most important signs of the Zodiac that can create an addiction. The house it is in will determine how that addiction will try to become fulfilled.

When someone is born with Venus in Capricorn, it can bring out a natural enjoyment of what a few other Venus sign positions consider kinky sex. Oral sex is not an uncommon act for this lover. This person may kiss you at any time, any place, passionately, or just a quick peck on the lips. It can be on the neck, hand, cheek, and yes, other thought provocative areas.

The male will have a strong protective instinct about their lover or mate, yet the women are perfectly able to get along by themselves. At the same time, this is not a lover to make angry with you, as they can be vindictive. Any involvement with a lover having this Venus location must be kept discreet, as this is a person who does not like social complications. That is, relationships outside of their normal domestic commitments must be kept quiet. Yet, when they are ready to make love, nothing else matters. Once this lover takes a mate, it is usually for life, as they normally choose carefully. The later in life this Venus position decides on a mate, the better chance of finding a soul mate, and the better the chance of marital survival. This person is often found with an older or younger mate. Ten years difference in ages is not uncommon.

VENUS IN AQUARIUS

This lover, loves the whole forest rather than one tree. With Venus in Aquarius you have a lover who is willing to share their love with several partners, and all will gain experience from each of the relationships. They may also wander from lover to lover in their affections.

If a prospective mate does not understand this lover's basic nature, marriage to this person may seem as if it was a drastic mistake. At the same time, this can be a lover who is very moral minded. The male may be almost Victorian in their treatment of the women in their lives.

The women with this Venus position are very friendly, almost to the point of using friendliness to replace love and sexuality. You cannot possess this Venus lover. If you attempt to do so, you will find yourself with a very rebellious lover, but not for long. Offer them freedom and they will stay. Try to fence them in and you will find the gate open, and they will be gone. This could be a partner to teach you new and different things. If it's unusual, they may like it, and will eagerly teach their newest lover.

Venus, in this sign, will bring with it a craving for something. This is one of the four most important signs of the Zodiac that can create an addiction. The house it is in, will determine how that addiction will try to become fulfilled.

VENUS IN PISCES

Persons born with this Venus position may seem to exhibit senseless emotions, emotions that can be frustrating for others they are involved with. Often, it may appear as though this person puts up little resistance to temptations that come their way. Their emotions may run the gamut as well. Both the male and female can crave emotional excitement as a sexual stimulant. Fantasy will be a prominent part of their love life, perhaps even to perversion. Promiscuity is not unheard of with Venus in Pisces. Remember this, too, is a dual sign.

This person will need to feel as though they have your total devotion toward them in the relationship. As someone with Venus in Pisces may not totally understand love and its many complications. They may also expect you, as a lover, to understand their love needs without telling you.

PERSONAL TIPS

Though this portion of the book is not about one's love life directly, it is some information you will find of interest. Becoming aware of people's hands can tell you a great deal about them personally. We are not going to discuss palmistry here, but the decorative manner in which people wear their jewelry, and what it can tell you about each individual. The following information may tell you how you might approach someone that appeals to you, with out any further personal knowledge of that person.

All things in life are influenced by one planet or another, and this includes the parts of your physical body. Each finger on our hands is, as well, ruled by a different planet, regardless of which hand. It is the jewelry worn on each finger that is foretelling.

Though it is rare, you will see people wearing rings on their thumbs. As the thumb is ruled by Mars, you can assume that a person wearing a ring on this finger is assertive, as an Aries might be. If you appeal to this person, they might make the first approach. If not, they will not mind if you approach them with an intimate offer first. In fact, the wearer of a thumb ring may find it stimulating to have someone else make the intimate play first.

A ring on the index finger, is someone who is very outgoing, and someone who trusts their own judgments. If you do not appeal to this person, odds are you will get no further than an introduction, no matter your endeavors. This is a sporty person so they are often in good physical shape. They will expect you to be able to keep up with them in any endeavor, and in their personal needs as well.

Rings on the middle finger are very interesting. This is someone who is a deep thinker, and someone who will be aroused by younger, or older, love partners. Ten years age difference is common for someone wearing a ring on this finger. If you are younger and become this person's lover, expect to be given lessons in lovemaking. If older, expect to be ravaged by the youth of your new lover, perhaps even to giving lessons in lovemaking. When you observe someone with rings on the middle finger, which is ruled by Saturn, and if they have a ring on their thumb as well, they will tend toward the younger lover. If there is no thumb ring, but there is a Saturn ring, the tendency will be toward the older lover.

The normal ring finger is ruled by Venus. This is a person who has an artistic ability in some manner. Is it in love making? This may be the lover, who enjoys wearing provocative clothing, and wearing it for any opportunity that might arise to showcase themselves.

The little finger, most often referred to as the 'Pinkie finger,' is the one to watch for rings if you are seeking a lover. A ring placed here shows a person of mentality, and one who enjoys learning. It also shows someone who understands the communications of love. This finger indicates interests in sexuality and lovemaking. Write them an erotic story and see where it leads.

There is a question, at this point, as I've not done enough research on the subject, but there may be a connection between those who wear tight bracelets, and an interest in bondage.

POINT OF SELF - *PS*

The Point of Self, as referred to in this book, is the location an individual in their life by age, this is in respect to the cycle of Uranus. To track the 'POINT of SELF' through the natal horoscope, you start with the first house cusp as the age of zero or, the beginning of life. The zero age position or, first house cusp, is considered the person's birth time in this cycle. Allowing for two years and four months for each house, you count around the chart, house by house, until the current age you are concerned with is found, or the age that has a relationship to the planet, or the house cusp in question. To find the actual place a person is by age, in any particular house of their chart, at any particular point in time, you will need to find out how many degrees and minutes are in that house. Convert the degrees to minutes and add that sum to the minutes already attributed to that house.

Example:
First house cusp = 12* Scorpio 16'
Second house cusp = 17* Scorpio 44'
The difference is   35* Scorpio 28' in the first house.

The degrees difference, times 60 minutes
$$35^* \times 60 = 2100'$$
Add the previous minutes from the chart. 28'
Total time in minutes.   2128'

Continue by dividing 2128 minutes by 28 months, which is (2 Years 4 Months).

2128' ÷ 28 = 76' per month of age, or 1* 16' = one month.

This being the case in this instance, you add one degree and sixteen minutes to the beginning of the first house cusp for each month of passage through the first house.

As the Point of Self passes through each house, it transmits the events of that house to the individual. So, when the point of self passes through the first, fourth, seventh, and tenth houses, the events are social encounters, in some manner.

When passing through the second, fifth, eighth, or eleventh houses, the events are more along the lines of physical encounters.

When the Point of self passes through the mental houses, three, six, nine and twelve, these are Cadent houses and may need to be closely watched as problems can arise while the person is going through this part of their life.

VIRGINITY LOST

You would not think you could tell about this time frame of life, and the potential of someone losing their virginity by just looking at their natal chart.

Yet, as with most of life's secrets, the stars can point the directions to nearly anything that has, or will take place. Well, to the eyes of untrained student, perhaps it will be a little more difficult, but there are some interesting points in a person's natal chart that can indicate the possibilities for the loss of their virginity, whether it is given, or taken. For most adults this might not seem to be a big deal, but that would depend on how your own virginity was relinquished. The ability to have access to this same information, for a parent, could be an eye opener.

You would think this a simple factor to observe, but it is not. There are many things to look for in a chart, such as each planet's position by sign and house. Perhaps one of the more prominent indicators is when the *Point of Self* is in an aspect to the more important planets, or houses. It can be conjunct by age to the natal Venus position, or it will be found making an aspect to the natal Venus.

Venus is the planet of love, but Neptune must be considered, as Neptune is the planet of deception and often plays a part in decisions concerning one's love life. It can also play a part in how someone is introduced into the sexual world, good or bad according to the aspect. Mars is another planet to keep an eye on, as it can indicate how the person will participate, or involve themselves in matters having to do with their sex life, or any avenues of life.

Yet, there are some potent influences when the Point of Self is in a conjunction to the first, fourth, seventh, or tenth house cusps. The reasons for becoming aware of these positions of the Point of Self, is because they are either in a conjunction to the first house, the physical body, or they are square, or in opposition to this very important physical house. These are generally the more prominent aspects that bring about an action, good, or bad.

The aspects to look for are listed below with the indicators used in this book.
  X 30* Semi-sextile
  ✶ 60* Sextile
  △ 120* Trine
  ∠ 45* Semi-square
  □ 90* Square
  ∞ 180* Opposition

Most of the time it will be the hard aspects of squares and oppositions which bring the astrological triggers into play for many of the sexual events in our lives. In some cases, they will not be enjoyable times.

The charts used in this book are personal lives, and, with that in mind, the reader must understand the birth data will not be included in this book. Because of that, these sample charts will not show the exact degrees and minutes, as the intention is to make the reader aware of where someone might be by age in their chart, and how these events can take place. Look to your own chart, and those you know on a personal basis, with some searching you will find the evidence of the events of which you search.

You should know this, but, in a man's chart, you would look to the Moon as his sexual partner, or partners, and in a woman's chart, you would look to the Sun as her sexual partner, or partners.

CHART 1A

The point of self was located in a conjunction to the Moon and a soft sextile aspect to Venus when the event took place at age seven in this chart. This was the potential trigger that set the events in motion leading to this individual losing his virginity to two sisters living across the street from his home. He was just under the age of seven. As you will see, the natal Moon resides in the third house, the third house representing the neighborhood in his community.

The Uranus to Moon conjunction, is in a squared aspect to Venus in the first house, and will have an effect on this individual for his entire life. He will, in effect, learn that he can talk women into bed as he wishes. The third house of communications, being squared to the first house of the personal pleasures of Venus, will bring these events to life. He will also learn, as life goes on, that he is a sexual addict.

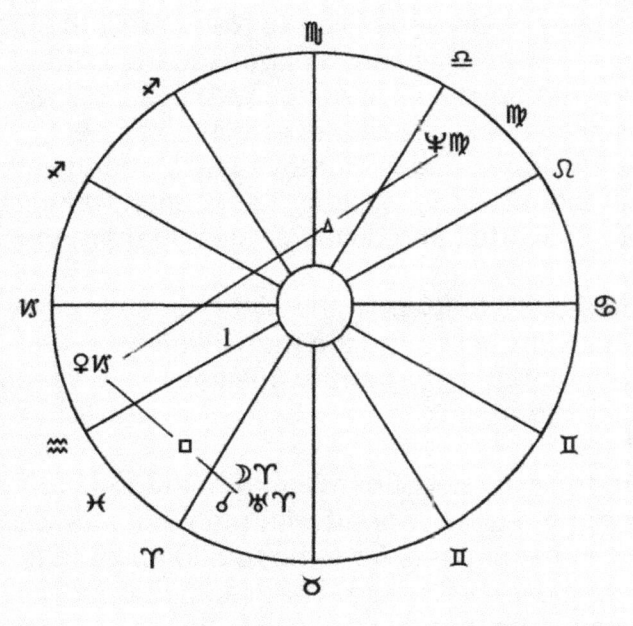

CHART 1A

CHART 2A

The point of self, and the rape, was at the age of fourteen, in an opposition to Neptune in the first house. Also, she was, by age, square to Mars in the ninth house. This brings with it, a life long restrictive sexual attitude, and it mixes her feelings toward sex. Her love life is often tainted with the memory of her first encounter, bringing with it, distrust and distaste, even in marriage.

The square to Mars in the ninth house imparted a negative reaction, as the man involved in the rape represented a trustworthy position. He was a man of the cloth.

The trine aspect of her Sun to her Moon can produce a good rapport with men, but she will see to it that she gains from the relationship, thus getting even with men. The Neptune opposition to the seventh house, and sextile to her Sun, may cloud her visions of the men she chooses during her life.

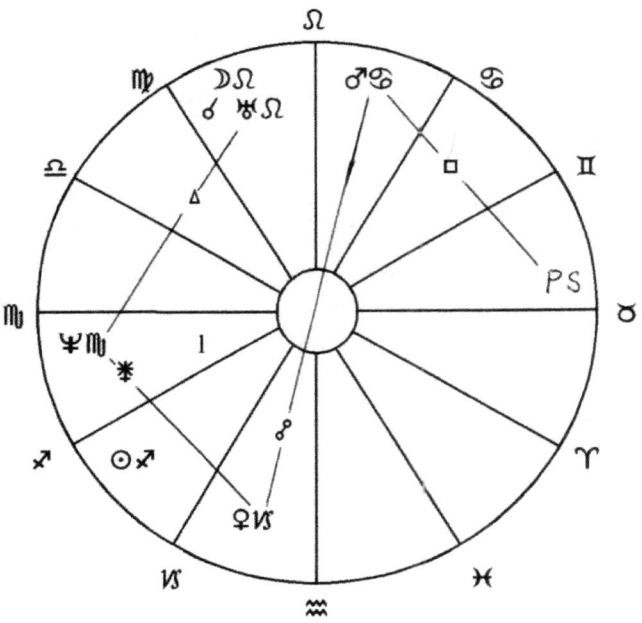

CHART 2A

CHART 3A

This young woman was introduced to the world of sexual love at the age of nineteen. Her Point of Self was Semi-sextile to her Moon in the tenth house of Career, it took place while she was gaining a college education for her chosen profession.

Her Sun, Venus, and Neptune in a conjunction in the seventh house were in opposition to her first house. Her Moon is sextile to the first house of her physical being, and squared her Sun. Venus and Neptune are in opposition to her intercepted sign of Aries in the first house, yet she gave herself willingly, mentally and physically.

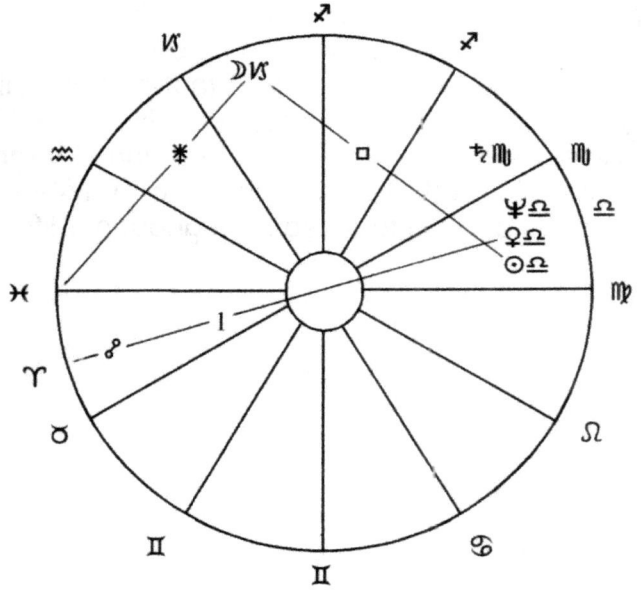

CHART 3A

CHART 4A
This teenager gave her virginity willingly at the age of fifteen, though her Point of Self was not conjunct her Venus at the time, it was in opposition to Neptune. Venus was also semi-sextile to her Point of Self. The Moon was Trine to Neptune and the ascendant. A four-planet stellium in Gemini in the tenth is squared to Neptune. The stellium in Gemini, squared to Neptune in Virgo, will have presented some unusual circumstances, and may continue to do so throughout her life.

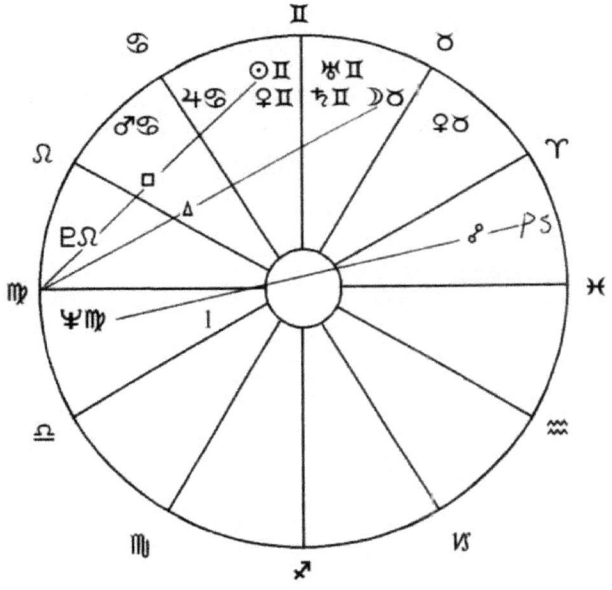

CHART 4A

Chart 5A
This teenage boy, was seduced by an older woman on a weekend camping trip. He was sixteen years old at the time. You can see the Moon is in opposition to his Venus. His age at point of self was square to both of these planets, but sextile to Neptune. The point of self formed a tee square at the age he lost his virginity. The older woman, and the situation, are shown by Saturn and Uranus in conjunction in Sagittarius in the fourth house. He gave of himself willingly.

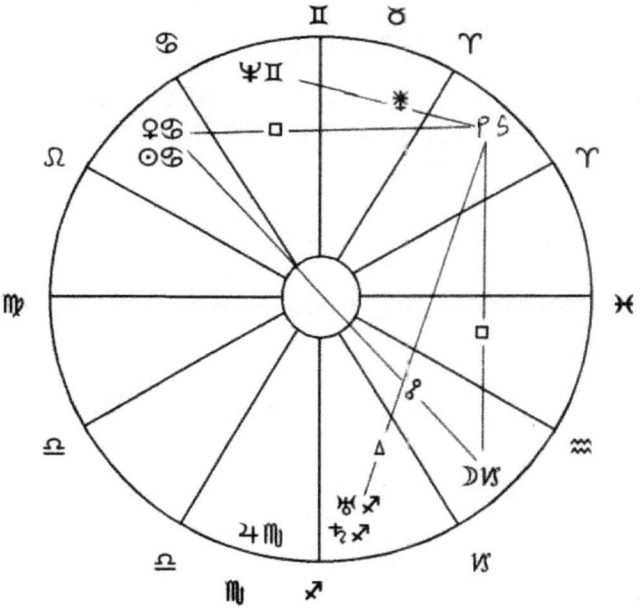

CHART 5A

CHART 6A

This girl was age six when she was raped and nearly beaten to death. Her Point of Self in the third house is conjunct Neptune, and in opposition to the natal Moon and Mars in the eighth house. The Moon and Mars are squared to Venus and Saturn in the eleventh house. The rape was by a friend of the father.

It wasn't until she crossed over the Point of Self again at the age of 34, that she felt she was able to finally tell someone about the rape. The third house of short distance travels, neighborhoods, and communications were involved each time. The rape took place in the back seat of her father's car while she waited for her father as he and his friend were drinking in a neighborhood bar.

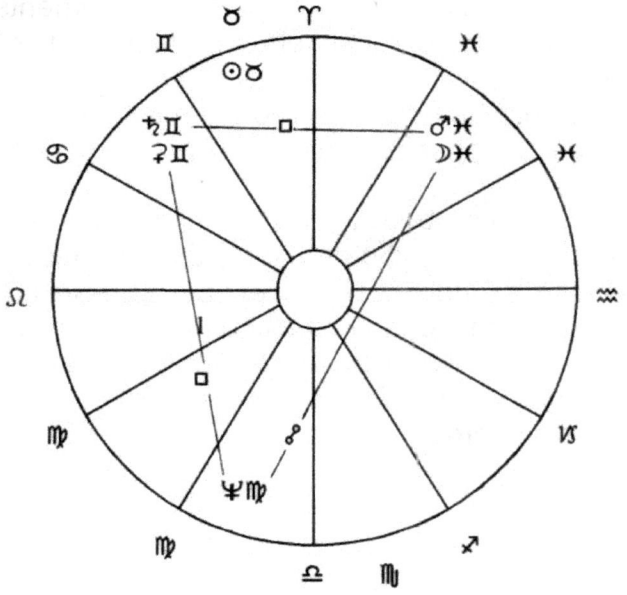

CHART 6A

PROBLEM PLANETS IN HOUSES

Not only is Venus a problem in some signs, it may also be more of a problem in some houses. Venus indicates where the love or enjoyments of life come into play. Remember, enjoyments often lead to an over indulgence in whatever gives us pleasure. The house position can tell you how those influences take place.

After reading about Venus in 'The Curses of Venus,' section, you can apply that information to each of the individual houses. Let's discuss the heavier natal house impacts of Venus first, and then we will review the remaining houses. As you read this, you will find the houses are not listed in sequential order.

VENUS IN THE FIRST HOUSE OF PERSONALITY

With Venus in the first house, the high sexual drive becomes more apparent. It is more difficult having Venus in this house because it is now a personal and a physical influence. Venus in any house will cause over indulgence in those related parts of life, but here in has to do with the individual's physical being and drive. Most of the problems encountered will involve the attitude and opinions of the person, and either of these can cause problems.

The attitude is that they want to fulfill their desires and cravings, regardless of the personal costs to their private or public life. Their opinion is that they can fulfill these cravings no matter the problems it may cause them, or those close to them.

The direction in which Venus searches for gratification can depend on whether it is the chart of a male or female, and the influence of the constellation it is in. The placement of the sun or moon in the natal chart will show the other directions of how Venus will spread her tentacles to engulf the rest of the chart's potential. In a woman's chart, whatever house the Sun resides in, is where her Venus will look for sexual gratification. In the male's chart, it will be where ever the Moon resides.

If the sexual cravings and desires are held in check, the effects of Venus can take place in other ways. Such as overeating, often a tool used to make oneself less appealing to the opposite sex, but furthers the actual need. Or, starving ones self to look better. Perhaps the use of alcohol or drugs if a water sign inhabits the first house cusp. Most often the individual will seek a solution that affects the physical body in some manner, and it will be done with pleasure in mind.

The cravings brought about because of a first house Venus, will be apparent when you wake in the morning and only end when you go to sleep at night. When you are addicted to food or drink it is all you think about, if it is sex, the same condition is true.

The restlessness can be overwhelming. This first house of the physical body can cause addiction to anything that will bring pleasure to the individual. It matters not what the addiction is composed of, or whether it is good or bad for a person. Even age has little effect, just because the body starts to slow down, as with an older person, the mind does not.

VENUS IN ARIES IN THE FIRST HOUSE

This may very well be the most assertive lover, one who will pursue their intended playmate with vigilance. This will not be a shy individual, if you are their intended desire, you will be made aware of their interest in you. Yet, they will not waste much time on a pursuit that seems to be lacking in mutual interest. This is a busy lover, one who jumps into a relationship quickly, and may look for another lover just as quickly.

VENUS IN SCORPIO IN THE FIRST HOUSE

Undoubtedly, you've heard of the Nymphomaniac. Well, the first house of physical body is where that person's Venus is likely to be found. Venus in Scorpio is bad enough, but in the first house it may be insatiable. Should you choose to spend time with this person, be aware most of it may be spent in bed, or something that serves the same purpose. If you choose this lover, and were wrong in doing so, you will find yourself way out of your league. This is a strong and intense lover.

VENUS IN CAPRICORN IN THE FIRST HOUSE
This is a very social sun sign, but love affairs with this person will have to be very discreet. This is someone who not only wants their cake, but a second helping, perhaps even a third. That is, relationships outside of their normal domestic commitments can, and often will, happen. There may be more than one going at the same time. When they are ready to make love nothing else matters.

VENUS IN AQUARIUS IN THE FIRST HOUSE
Venus in Aquarius is the last of these four heavier sexual signs of the Zodiac. Aries, Scorpio, Capricorn, and Aquarius. With Aquarius being such a free thinker, and someone who thinks everyone deserves equal treatment, they give of themselves.

And, yes, they give themselves to lovers. But not to just anyone.

VENUS IN THE THIRD HOUSE

This house location of Venus can show a love of travel and communicating, such as writing novels or short stories. It will also involve a variety of individuals in this person's love life. The love experiences could come from their travels abroad, or at home. This is the house ruled by Gemini, hence duality. In this case, the duality may take its pleasure from several sources.

The third house love life can be very close to home, and very personal, which is where brothers and sisters come into play. Yes, that includes adopted brothers and sisters, even cousins. The third house rules relatives, and with Venus in the third house it can also bring about unwanted attention from a step parent. Outside of the personal home life, the Venus effect may include love affairs with an acquaintance, such as a neighbor.

This Venus position can provide a person with the ability to acquire knowledge, and this knowledge can find its way onto the written page. Very possibly it will add to their bank account.

VENUS IN THE TWELFTH HOUSE

The twelfth house Venus concerns hidden things, things that are kept hidden by the people involved, such as cheating on one's mate, but it can go much deeper than that. The problem most often encountered is that for some reason, we as individuals, cannot keep our mouths shut. If we have a secret love affair we will tell someone else about it, then our unknown love life will soon be known by someone else, and of course it doesn't stop there. Pride in our ability to attract the opposite sex can be costly.

With secret love affairs, the people involved are faced with a constant stream of lies and the fear of getting caught, and of course being found out is usually the end result. In a sense, those involved inform on themselves. Love affairs bring trouble for this Venus position, sometimes danger is also close at hand. It requires an unusual understanding between the two lovers to avoid a serious social downfall. A secure knowledge between them that this thing they have going is strictly an affair, and nothing else. That there is no long term plans to divorce their current mates, and ultimately to wed one another. Though this does happen.

The successful Venus in the twelfth house love affair takes place with the understanding that they both know this is for the fun of enjoying a different lover for the time. In the end, the secret love affair caused by Venus being placed in the twelfth house will come to an end. If it is a controlled love affair, as mentioned above, it will end without total unhappiness, and the destruction of two entire families.

One last thing to consider as a curse of Venus in this house, is that prostitution can take over the love life and direct the individual to a whole new lifestyle. This of course brings many unhappy situations to bear, and the diseases that can get passed along may only be the tip of the iceberg. Those who enjoy bondage and masochism, often have Venus in this house, or a suffering in some manner, something that is not brought out into the public eye. This life style, when one gets caught up in it, can truly be a curse.

There is a downside to Venus in this house, it can indicate someone who has difficulty reaching an orgasm. Whether it is caused by a physical condition, or something that happened to them in an earlier age. If it happened between the ages of twelve and fourteen counseling may be required to help them overcome the mental outlook.

VENUS IN THE FIFTH HOUSE

This is the house that rules love, it is also the house of children, your own, or those you adopt. Also it is the house of romances, with your spouse or with someone else's. You guessed it, this can be the house of promiscuity, a personal problem that can last a lifetime. A person with Venus here can fight the tendency, but, depending on the sign Venus is in at birth, it may be a losing battle.

Let's discuss some of the basics here and then an explanation of how things can just suddenly happen when two destined warm and open Auras cross paths with one another. This position of Venus brings with it a great deal of ongoing social events.

There is a tendency to gamble, or to take chances of some kind. Lovers can easily come from this house, as well as any kind of sensuous enjoyments. Sexuality is fully enjoyed by this person and it can involve sexual relationships in, or out, of the home. So, what can happen? Well, to begin with, this is a social person because of the placement of the planet of love, in the house of love.

Consider a social gathering taking place, and he/she meets a new person while mingling with the various guests. They start to talk, and the two of them enjoy the other person being close. Confidently they look each other over, and neither of them minds the potential lover's scrutiny.

After all, it is a sensuous experience, and they both enjoy the thought. After some flirting words are spoken, they agree to have lunch together. Would tomorrow be okay?

Okay, Monday for sure. This is a chance they both take, but more so for the person with Venus in the fifth house, hence the reason for the lunch. The person with Venus in the fifth house is gambling that the other person will be interested in fooling around. Monday comes, as does lunch, they sit next to each other, not across from one another at the table. Their legs are touching, their hands meet, perhaps under the table at first. After a brief discussion concerning their sexual likes and dislikes, they arrange to meet each other at a motel next Monday. He arranges for the room, and when she gets there, she goes into the bathroom, and when she comes out, she may be wearing a very transparent 'Teddy,' if anything.

This is a Venus position that can also bring out jealousy of one's mate, and perhaps self-indulgence of one sort or another.

VENUS IN THE REMAINING HOUSES.

VENUS IN THE SECOND HOUSE

Venus indicates an enjoyment for whatever house or sign it is in. As the second house is monetary, the enjoyment will be for financial well being. This can be a personal drive that can upset other family members. It will do so because of the drive to obtain whatever it is they want, matters so much to the individual that it can consume them. Probably the most important thing to this kind of person is the monetary freedom they know exists. No matter how it comes about, this person wants it for their own. This is a person who may marry just to enjoy the wealth of the marital partner. The importance here is in material possessions. Be it homes, cars, or anything of value. Will this person enjoy it? You can bet they will try. Will someone with this Venus position be rich? Perhaps, but probably not.

Odds are that once they get the financial means to do as they want, they will not give it away to anyone else on purpose. This financial freedom may come about through their personal endeavors, or it could just as easily come from the death of a partner, business or marital. You might think of someone with this kind of outlook as a cold and calculating person, but this is not necessarily the case. The second house is often thought of as a sexually stimulated house as well.

It should not surprise you to find that this person will have a hidden safe in their house somewhere. It may contain some kind of negotiable assets like stocks and bonds, or it could just as well have a box full of precious stones inside. You'll never know about it until they are gone from this world.

Another factor is that this house also rules the first born child. This will bring out a protective inclination from the parent, perhaps more so than for other children in the same family.

VENUS IN THE FOURTH HOUSE

A fourth house Venus is one of interest as it covers some unusual items, but mostly it is about the home, and the home life. It is concerned with the individuals personal home, or that of family estates. With Venus here, the living conditions will reflect the pleasures that the owner enjoys most. Among other things, there will be an area, somewhere in the home, that keeps any of the personal secrets, or belongings of its occupants, safely hidden away.

This person's intimate thoughts and concerns, may reflect the fact that they feel any older person in their family, should be allowed to live in the home with the younger family. This could be anyone from and aunt or an uncle, to one's parents and at least older family members. The living conditions for the elderly person will be greatly improved by this relationship.

Venus in this house can indicate losses caused by, or through children, or losses from a love affair that has ended badly. These love affairs, may have been an unstable affair in the beginning, as this Venus position encounters strange events in love and marriage.

VENUS IN THE SIXTH HOUSE

Venus in the sixth house can bring a discovery, and the enjoyment of doing things for others. Often to the point of self-denial. Is the self-denial something the individual consciously desires, of course not, but this person is someone who thinks about the needs of others. This, is a person who thinks that others need help before they actually get around to doing things for themselves.

You may see indications of them thinking this way and not recognize it right away. Such as a grandparent who living on a fixed income. Most of the time they can barely pay their own housing costs, and their medications put a tremendous strain on their bank account, if they have one. Yet, if there is a grandchild in need of a pair of shoes, the child will have them. Never mind how many meals the cost of the shoes may have provided for the grandparents. If it isn't grandchildren they are spending their money on, it could just as easily be animals, large or small. The animals will be spoiled, just as if they were grandchildren. New horseshoes for the horses, shots for the cats or dogs. A cat or dog will have a very plush bed to sleep in, even if they seldom use it for that purpose. Whatever emotional project it is, that sucks the lifeblood away from this person, it will enjoy the comforts of love.

More so in youth than in later years, with Venus in this house sexually transmitted diseases may have to be considered, and dealt with at some point in life. Of course, it can be expensive to suffer this malady, perhaps as high as costing a marriage.

VENUS IN THE SEVENTH HOUSE

Venus makes friends' where ever it resides at the time of your birth. When Venus is found in the seventh house, it brings out alliances that result in odd circumstances.

The relationships can be between women friends, or men friends, or perhaps it is just conjugal affections between two people, rather than a passionate love affair between sweethearts. The new relationship may start with a simple chance meeting involving a perfect stranger, yet a meeting that blossoms and grows much farther, and faster, than expected.

Something to think about is the fact that when Venus is in the seventh house it is also in opposition to the first house, which represents the person to whom the chart belongs. What this amounts to, is that the person may work against themselves by becoming involved in love affairs that may not be good for them.

If you are involved in one of these kind of relationships, take care in how you part company, as Venus in this house can result in personal enemies in the long run.

Secret relationships between two lovers will often result in divorce between them and their marital mates. More often than not, this will be done to change life's partners, rather than divorcing to satisfy the anger of the current mate.

This kind of relationship can result in a divorce that catches the marital partner completely off guard. The surprise comes because the marital partner may have felt all was well in his or her personal relationship.

VENUS IN THE EIGHTH HOUSE

The problems caused by Venus in this house will depend largely upon which sign Venus is in. As this, is the house that rules the sexual organs, it is a strong sexual house to begin with. Then you add a heavy Venus, such as Venus in Aries, Scorpio, or Capricorn, and you have a power to be reckoned with. The eighth house also rules the end of things and can contribute to the ending of relationships, marital or business. Someone with Venus in the eighth house may end up paying alimony for years because of the infidelities starting from a sexual affair.

The kind of relationships that can form from this Venus position will often be with friends from the past part of your life. Perhaps someone you were intimate with as a younger person suddenly shows up, and you get together for lunch, or dinner. The first thing you know it's having breakfast together, well you see where this is going.

There is a side to Venus being in this house that is often overlooked. Ones love life can come to an end here as well. It may simply be an age factor when the point of self reaches this house. Or a harsher side may result in someone's being in a relationship where the partner simply stops participating in the sexual act. It can also indicate someone who finds it difficult to enjoy sex.

VENUS IN THE NINTH HOUSE

This is not a house of high sexual needs, but with Venus residing here in the natal chart, it can still be a problem. Venus in this house may bring a love to travel, and not just around the neighborhood. Countries, and continents yes. This exploring may be disguised as something leading to a higher education, or it may be that the person just likes to travel.

This condition can bring with it some strange, or secret love affairs. The problem arises when the Venus travel effect, affects the family life, as this person is never home to take care of their home love life. This being the case, while they are gone, their loved ones may be doing a bit of exploring on their own. Searching for someone, who will be around in the evenings and weekends.

It doesn't have to be a traveler who is never home, it could just as easily be someone studying on a continual basis. As an example, it could be someone who is just beginning a career in the legal circles. Lawyers are notorious for spending endless hours at the office, all in the name of profession, and career. It doesn't have to be a student of Law, it can be any form of higher learning. A science of some kind, perhaps even that of a teacher who spends hours correcting tests, or getting the next class material ready for the upcoming class and the students.

Even publishers fall under the spell of this house, or writers who are trying to break into the published world. There are writers, who though working at home, seem distant from the family. It takes a steadfast mate to endure being a writer's widow, or widower. The writer may be present physically, but their minds are some where else most of the time

VENUS IN THE TENTH HOUSE

The tenth house Venus is, or can be, another form of promiscuity. The career, or profession takes place first, then the family may come next. The ambition for advancement is expensive in the terms of ones love life.

There is every indication there will be an office affair, these too, can be expensive in some manner. You have to pay the price eventually; it is only a matter of which it is you want to keep the family, or the career. If the rewards in the profession can result in fame, the family may have to wait, as the spotlight is hard to turn your back on.

Life can be tough on this kind of individual, because they think their mates do not understand them. It is this person, who has to make up their mind as to their goals in life, and its costs to them personally.

VENUS IN THE ELEVENTH HOUSE

Venus here is seldom a problem, unless one's mate is suffering from emotional neglect, as the lack of a loving companion does take a toll. It could be that this is a person who gives all of their love to children. Perhaps personal acquaintances, or other friendly companions, rather than giving it to their own mate. This may also be the mate who creates love problems into the marriage. Perhaps it's simply because they lack the knowledge to figure out what their own mate needs in the way of love, and, or affections. It is not unusual for someone with Venus in the eleventh house to marry into a ready-made family.

PROBLEM PLANETS IN THE SEVENTH HOUSE

The planets we discuss in this section do not necessarily cause problems themselves alone, but when coupled by aspect with other planets, they can create trouble in someone's life. It is this basic planetary nature; we will go over in this portion of the book.

It is the aspects from other planets in the chart to planets in the seventh house that are of importance. One of the problems of planets in the seventh house is that you may not see the harsh effects of the planet until after you marry, or form a partnership of some kind with these people. If you should end up with a partner who has one of these conditions in their chart, it can seem a cursed situation.

Sometimes the biggest problems arise from planets located in the first or twelfth houses. The first house because it affects the personal side of the individual as well as the physical. The twelfth house because it brings out hidden things. These hidden things can produce dramatic influences in any relationship.

SUN

The Sun in the seventh house can produce a partner who may be domineering. Perhaps even selfish, or too extravagant in their life style. If you marry someone who has the Sun in the seventh house as a step toward a higher social standing, it can be a very expensive step.

When comparing the seventh house Sun and the other planets that are in an opposition aspect, there may no problems associated with the Moon, Venus, or Neptune, but, if possible, even these should be in good aspects.

A person who has the Sun in the seventh house may not marry until later in life, this happens often because of the fires that burn within. A feeling can reside in this person that prevents them from settling down to a fixed lifestyle.

MOON

The aspects between the Moon and the other planets in the chart are of importance. If you choose someone with the Moon in the seventh house, you may find yourself with a moody partner. This can also be a partner who will possibly stray from the marital bed.

This is a good position for a parent with children in the home, but it can make the partnership a real problem. This may bring a mate who is greedy and ready to take anything within reach. As the ruler of the Sun sign Cancer, the Moon can bring a partner into your life, who nags you a great deal of the time. Perhaps one who insists that you agree with his or her line of thinking. Often, a partner in this kind of relationship will give in, just to keep the peace.

The Moon in this house of one's horoscope does not indicate a successful marriage the first time. The second marriage will have a better chance at survival.

MERCURY

Remember, this is the planet of communication we are discussing here, and with this planet in the seventh house it can produce a partner who is talkative and flirtatious. Yet, their mind will remain true to the marriage, and to the marital partner.

Mercury in this house can produce a mate who is younger, perhaps even a distant relative, or a past school friend. Either of these conditions will bring their relatives influence into the family as well.

If you have Mercury in this house and if the aspects to Mercury are harsh aspects, you can attract a partner who is constantly talking, or nagging. Make your decision before the union takes place, as Mercury in this position can produce a relationship where steady bickering, or quarreling is commonplace. Those same aspects can cause problems should a divorce start to take place. If this is the case, you, as the marital partner, may want to guard your bank account. It could disappear quickly if left unguarded.

VENUS

If Venus has good aspects while in this house, it will be a very good indication of a warm and loving relationship. If, Venus has bad aspects while in this house, it can bring a disappointing mate into your life. Among other things this is not a neat and tidy type person.

If, Venus is in one of the fire signs, Aries, Leo, or Sagittarius, it may bring with it a partner who has a detached view towards the marriage. In the case of Leo, it can be the best of the fire signs for Venus to be in, in the seventh house. Venus in Aries can be a mate who requires a mate to keep up with, or meet their sexual needs.

Venus in Pisces, Cancer, or Taurus, in the seventh house, may be the best astrological signs for compatibility in the marriage.

MARS

The planet Mars in the seventh house can bring about spontaneous, and irregular love affairs. Mars in this house can also cause arguments, perhaps even accidents, or disruptions of any kind. In short, this is not a good planet to have in the seventh house. If a nearly fatal accident occurs, look to the aspects to Saturn. If Saturn is involved, a similar accidental situation can occur again in 7 years 3 months. Also at 14 years and 6 months later. These are not the exact dates but they will be close.

Mars here can attract a partner to you who may seem ideal, but more often Mars brings with it a danger to the person who has Mars in their seventh house. If Mars is in a water sign in your seventh house, you may be someone who is constantly drawn to partners who drink excessively. If this is the case in your natal chart, you may be the one who has been heard to say, "Why do I always choose this kind." Well Mars in a water sign is the reason, and it will seem like an ongoing curse.

JUPITER

To set up a marriage chart with the intention of having the planet Jupiter as a beneficial planet in the seventh house, can be an error. Though, as a rule in the marital chart, or the natal chart, it does bring some ability to protect the individual, and the marriage. However, it has squares and opposition aspects in the natal chart, it can bring about not only bad luck, but in some cases, tremendous misfortune. A badly aspected Jupiter will often allow the individual to choose the wrong mate for their life. It can also indicate someone who will have numerous affairs of the heart, before, during, and after marriage. If Jupiter is in the seventh house, and if possible, you want it to have good aspects to the Sun, Moon, and the planet ruling the ascending sign.

SATURN

This can be a problem planet for any seventh house partnership. Saturn in this house, can, and often does, cause the loss of a mate, perhaps even denying marriage for some years. A normal reaction in life is that when Saturn is found in the natal chart's seventh house, it brings about a marriage between two people who have a large difference in ages between them. Ten years is quite common, and twenty years difference can happen as well. Often this relationship starts when the planet Venus is transiting through a sign quite compatible to both partners. This is only a curse if the age difference causes some end of life problems for the mate left to fend for him, or herself.

It can just as easily bring a marital union in which one of the partners is of a cold nature. If this is the case, the one with the natal Saturn in the seventh house, should consider getting a divorce. Good luck if this is the case, because; this may be a marital partner who refuses, for one reason or the other, to agree to a divorce.

URANUS

One of the dangers of having Uranus in the seventh house is the odd, or unusual circumstances surrounding the possible mate chosen. Uranus in this house does not really favor marriage, as it instills a certain need for freedom from restrictions of any kind. Though the partner chosen is often above average in intelligence, and may understand the others needs. This planet is more favorable to marriage when placed in a woman's seventh house rather than a man's, because in a man's chart it can bring a possibility of homosexuality. If Uranus is badly aspected, you can expect the marriage to fall apart, and why would anyone stay together when neither of them can be happy?

NEPTUNE

Does this person seem happy in their marriage? It may seem so to others, but we are dealing with Neptune here. Odds are, there will be some dissatisfaction in the marriage, whether the conditions causing the problems are real, or imagined. The person with Neptune in the seventh house, is often someone who self sacrifices themselves for the mate, at least that can be the way they see the situation. Their mate may be someone who is pitied, perhaps needs to be nursed through the years, even locked away somewhere. When the wrong kind of marriage is entered into, it can be a total waste. Normally this marriage will end, and rightly so.

This is the planet of deception, and it can produce a marital partner that may seem unknown, even to the mate. The real person with this Neptune position may never be truly known to their mates, or anyone else. It is not unusual for this marital partner to desert the marriage without explanation, or prior notice. The old saying of 'Here today, gone tomorrow,' can easily fit this Neptune placement.

PLUTO

Pluto usually shows a need, so when you find someone with Pluto in the seventh house, it indicates a person needs a mate in their life. With Pluto in this house, it can bring someone into the relationship that seems sensuous in their very nature. Pluto in this house can change a mate from a stick in the mud, to an erotic lover. Pluto is a planet which brings changes, and generally for the better.

LOVERS OF THE SIXTH and TWELFTH HOUSE

The Astrological signs that fall on the sixth and twelfth house cusps of a chart, are good, or bad, depending on how, or when they begin to effect a persons life. Both the sixth and twelfth houses are restrictive houses; thus, both Sun signs that fall on these house cusps can be restrictive signs to the native. Generally, relationships with people of these signs are trouble from the beginning, though at the time one may not think of them as such. But once you cross some line, and only they know where it is, all hell can break loose. As a rule these are two Sun signs a person should not get involved with for long term relationships. Short term, associations may work out, but don't bet on it.

Look at your own personal chart, and remember that communications between yourself and the people who are of the Sun signs found on your sixth and twelfth houses, may be misunderstood. Perhaps even wantonly disregarded, either of which can cause complicated problems later. Most of the time an intimate relationship with one of the Sun signs found on the twelfth house will not normally be known about, as they will be hidden relationships from the beginning. The problems that can be caused are not openly known by many of those acquainted with the two people involved. But complications can arise that will be demanding in some manner.

The sign on the sixth house can cause problems as well, but these relationships will come before the public's eye in some manner. You would think any problems caused by the sign on the twelfth house would be seen by the public as well because it is closer to the Midheaven, but this is not the case. However, the sign on the sixth house seems to demand some public attention.

With Neptune as the ruler of the twelfth house, it will color, or disguise the reality of the relations. Mercury, ruler of the sixth house, will communicate the displeasure of the relationship. Aspects from the natal Sun, and Moon to the rulers of these two house cusps will tell much of the story about the negative, or positive, relationships of the man and woman involved.

When you consider that there are usually two signs to contend with in each house, The one on the opening cusp, and the one on the ending cusp, or the opening cusp of the following house, each will have some influence in the chart. Looking at your chart, you will have to consider that the last of one sign and the beginning of the other sign may not be good for you.

If you are contemplating a relationship with someone who has Venus in this house be sure you are familiar with any mental baggage they may have been carrying for years.

EXPLANATION CHART 3B

Looking at chart 3B, you can see that anyone whose Sun sign falls between 25* Virgo 24' and 9* Leo 16', can be a restriction of some sort to this person. It would be the same situation for the signs on the sixth and seventh house cusps as well, 25* Pisces 24', and 9* Aquarius 16'.

There are those who feel that relationships that take place with the sun signs on these houses, often go as unfinished love affairs. As if love affairs between the charts individual and the signs on these two houses may also be fated Karma love affair. It is as if they develop a relationship that will, or can, only be completed in another life time. It's as the Sun signs found on these house cusps can be like a candle flame and a moth. The fire keeps burning, drawing the moth closer, and closer though danger lurks.

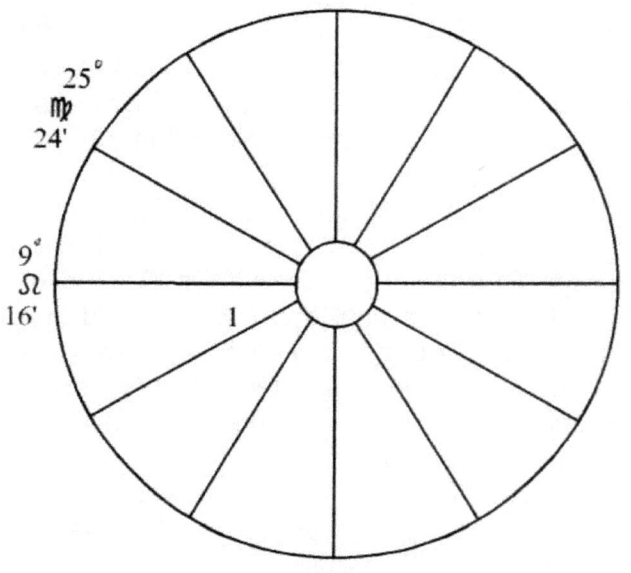

CHART 3B

SEXUAL GENDER INFLUENCES OF THE SUN SIGNS

Each sign of the Zodiac has some influence as to gender control over the native's chart at the time of birth. Following is a list of the constellations and their gender influence. However, this does not mean that a man with several planets in feminine signs, will exhibit female tendencies, but it may mean he will understand, and get along better with women than many other men.

The same is true of a woman with several planets in masculine signs. She may not seem quite as feminine as other women, but she will not be any less a woman. Perhaps, this will be the girl who is a tomboy as a child, then as she gets older she will understand men, and their needs, more than other women do. In the end, she may have the better relationship with men, a relationship other men and women can only desire.

Aries. . . . .Masculine
Taurus . . .Feminine
Gemini . . .Masculine
Cancer . . .Feminine
Leo. . . . . .Masculine
Virgo. . . . .Feminine

Libra. . . . . . .Masculine
Scorpio. . . . .Feminine
Sagittarius . .Masculine
Capricorn . . Feminine
Aquarius. . .Masculine
Pisces . . . . .Feminine

The Femininity, or Masculinity of the planets.

Mars . . . . Masculine	Jupiter . . . . Masculine
Venus . . . Feminine	Saturn . . . . Feminine
Mercury. . Androgyne	Uranus . . . Masculine
Moon . . . Feminine	Pluto. . . . . Feminine
Sun . . . . . Masculine	Neptune . . Feminine

Androgyne - can be either male or female, but often considered as Masculine.

Masculine planets that fall into masculine signs are apt to be much more masculine, than if they fall into feminine signs. The same would be true of the feminine planets when they fall into feminine signs.

SEXUAL INTERESTS OF THE SUN SIGNS

To a few readers, the following information will hold little interest, but it will be very few. Most students of life want to understand themselves, and they want to know about their friends, or the person they just met. A few may be surprised to learn they are not so unusual after all.

This next section does not require you to have an astrological chart on someone, but that information would help you to better understand the whole person. You must remember these are only the Sun sign influences. A number of planets in any other sign, can cloud these same influences, or add more. You will want to consider the ascending sign as well, as it rules the personality, and the physical being.

Most of the following items pretty well explain themselves, but one heading, 'Kinky sex,' is comprised of several different items. Such as Bondage, Sadomasochism, Masochism, Ménage À Trois, sexual orgies, etc. The following are listed alphabetically.

Affairs while involved with someone else, single or married.
>Aries, Taurus, Gemini, Scorpio, Sagittarius, Aquarius, Pisces.

Anal sex may be enjoyed.
>Cancer, Scorpio, Sagittarius

Bisexual Potential.
>Gemini, Libra, Sagittarius, Sometimes Capricorn, Pisces.

Can be cool towards sex, but surprises do happen.
>Gemini, Virgo.

Dominating roll may be played, and can be enjoyed.
>Aries, Cancer, Virgo, Scorpio.

Breasts being fondled induce pleasure.
>Taurus, Cancer, Pisces.

Exhibitionism.
>Leo, Libra, Pisces, Aquarius.

Fantasizes.
> Gemini, Cancer, Leo, Virgo, Libra, Scorpio Pisces.

Often those birth charts that contain planets in Virgo, will fantasize.

Homosexual or Lesbian inclinations.
> Sometimes Taurus,
> Sometimes Virgo, Sagittarius.

Incestuous interests, or potential involvement's.
> Leo, Aquarius, Cancer, Capricorn.

Kinky sex. Look at the aspect relationship between Venus and Mars, Saturn, Neptune and Pluto. You may want to keep handcuffs, soft rope, Dildos, or other items this lover enjoys, handy. The Sun, representing men, or, the Moon representing women, may be located in the twelfth house.
> Taurus, Leo, Virgo, Libra, Scorpio, Sagittarius.

Likes being the partner on top while love making.
> Aries, Leo, Scorpio, Capricorn.

Makes noises while enjoying sex.
    Aries, Taurus, Leo, Sagittarius, Capricorn.

Prefers to make love in the,
Mornings   Afternoons   Evenings   Anytime
    Aries   Virgo   Sagittarius

Making love outside is stimulating.
    Taurus, Gemini, Cancer, Scorpio, Sagittarius.

Masturbates
    Aries, Taurus, Cancer, Virgo, Scorpio, Sagittarius, Aquarius, Pisces.

Monogamous relationships are preferred.
    Leo, Virgo.

Nymphomania. This often depends on the sign Venus inhabits, but the more common are.
    Taurus, Scorpio

Oral sex is enjoyed, receiving or bestowing.
    Gemini, Cancer, Leo, Scorpio, Sagittarius, Capricorn, Aquarius.

Pornographic stories, or films are enjoyed.
    Taurus,   Leo,   Scorpio,
    Sagittarius   Aquarius,   Pisces.

Promiscuous behavior.
    Gemini,   sometimes Cancer,
    Sagittarius,   Sometimes Aquarius.

Sexual toys, and this may be any kind of stimulant.
    Aries,   Taurus,   Gemini,
    Virgo,   Pisces.

Talking dirty turns them on, depending on the time and location.
    Gemini,   Sagittarius.

Uses sex.
    Gemini,   Scorpio,   Capricorn.

SPECIAL NOTES

In my discussions with those who enjoy bondage, I found that the fantasies they favor, or prefer to read about, involve submission. One of the more prominent reasons for the need to be submissive is often because they themselves are domineering, or controlling individuals in their normal daily lives.

Being submissive removes their control, and gives their lovers the manipulative power. A role reversal that they enjoy as they are placed at the mercy of someone else. The thought of being ravished by their lover, with no control on their part, other than an agreement of how far to go, is the sexual high. In some cases, reaching a climax without this kind of love making, is difficult.

The planets involved are Saturn, Mars, Venus and the luminary representing their gender. That is the Moon for women, and the Sun for men. Often that luminary planet can be found in the twelfth house at the time of birth. The closer to the ascendant, the more powerful the influence.

THE SEXUAL HOUSES

The sexual houses are the fixed houses, 2 5, 8, and 11. They involve insecurities, possessions, and self esteem. The fifth house is the house of love and children. The eighth house rules the sexual organs and the end of things. There is no question of these two houses being prominent in someone's love life. However, the opposite houses, the second and the eleventh, also have some influence in ones love life. We will use chart '1B' as an example chart, and the information, as written, is not in numerical order. You would delineate your own chart in a similar fashion. The signs on each of these houses could reveal a possible mate, it is up to you to find the one best suited to your needs.

THE SECOND HOUSE

The second house has some physical influence in the chart because of its opposition to the eighth house, which is ruled by the planet Pluto, and is the ruler of the sex organs. If you have a natal chart on yourself, look at the sign constellation on the second house cusp. The sign appearing here, will be one of physical attraction.

Using the 'chart 1B' you will see this male has Libra on the second house, so he will be sexually attracted to women born in the sign of Libra.

THE FIFTH HOUSE

The fifth house is the house of love and of children. There is no question the sign on this house can be one of sexual attraction. The male of chart 1B will be attracted physically to the Sun sign of Capricorn appearing on his fifth house cusp. Capricorn, ruled by Saturn, can, in this case, represent older women. This man will be attracted to older women partially because his first love was older than himself and she was his first teacher in the art of lovemaking.

THE EIGHTH HOUSE

This is another sexual, and physical house, perhaps the one with the most influence. With Aries on his eighth house cusp, this male will also be attracted to Aries women, and he himself may be assertive in his search for women in his life. This house is squared to his Venus and Moon, which will enhance his assertiveness. In some cases, this assertion may scare off a potentially good mate.

THE ELEVENTH HOUSE

The last of the fixed houses, and of physical attraction, and this male has Cancer on this house cusp. Because he is a Cancer Sun sign, he may be drawn to a Cancer female to fill his home life. He definitely yearns for a home and the peace and quiet it offers; yet, he will encounter some problems in this respect. His Virgo ascendant influence may expect it to be a perfect home life. It won't be, because he can't take it with him, as he is a traveling writer.

PLANETARY ASPECTS

Though planetary aspects can, and do trigger many of the problems in our love lives. However, the unsettling conditions will not take place unless the planets themselves are in signs and houses that bring the charts potential into play during the persons lifetime. All of this depends upon the time of birth. Is that a coincidence, or is it planned before birth?

If you are not familiar with the signs and symbols, a table containing the names of the signs, their symbols, and the aspects, can be found near the end of this book.

Perhaps you're wondering how life can be planned before a child's birth. You are most likely aware there are many people who feel we, as human beings, plan our next lives according to a Karmic debt, or a Karmic need. This can be an interesting area for discussion, but we'll not go into it further here.

As most students of Astrology understand, aspects, which are the relationships between two planets, can cause certain events to take place. Or they may offer some potential to the individual who has the aspects in question. Truthfully, I'm not sure which is more powerful, trines or squares, I am however, sure they are misunderstood by many new students of this wonderful science.

In the beginning of our astrological studies, we are taught that square aspects are bad, and that trine aspects are good. Often this is a reversed situation in life. That is, squares can be good because they allow a person to take action in their lives as needed, and as long as the power is used in a positive manner.

△Trines are only good if they are used correctly, but they are often taken for granted, and left to take care of the events as needed. When this happens, the individual does little to push him or herself ahead in life when the opportunity presents itself. It can be the same for oppositions, or conjunctions. Though, these aspects can actually hold more power than the squares or trines.

□ Square aspects can easily form Tee squares, and grand crosses to any opposition aspect in the chart. Suppose you have a planet in the first and seventh houses, they would be in opposition to each other, now add a planet in the fourth and tenth houses; they to are in opposition to each other. The planet in the first house is squared to the planet in the fourth house, and it is squared to the planet in the seventh, which creates a tee square. The planet in the seventh house is squared to the planet in the tenth; thus, a grand cross is formed.

It often happens, that a chart can have grand trines as well. Again, suppose you have a planet in the first house, one in the fifth house, and one in the ninth house. Each is trine to the other, and three of them form a grand trine.

♀ The conjunction aspect can easily pull another planet into play that may have been left dormant on its own. Resulting in the planet's ability to function in its normal manner, yet in such a way as suggested by the aspects to the planet it is in conjunction with. So, what happens to one planet, happens to the other one as well. Another factor is that the conjunction can be part of an opposition, or grand trine. The behavior of the conjunction can be from a relaxed situation, to a radical course of action.

CHART 1A

With chart 1A we'll discuss how some of the problems in our love life can come into play, and some of the other planetary influences in an individual's chart, as nothing happens by chance. In this chart we have a man who has Venus in Capricorn in the first house. From the Venus curses section, we find that this is a very lustful Venus position. Venus in Scorpio would be worse, in Aries would be slightly less, and even if it was in Aquarius, it would have some affect.

As Capricorn is ruled by the planet Saturn, this person will gravitate to younger or older lovers, or life mates. Ten years difference in ages is not unusual. The age difference is attributed to the Saturn influence as the ruler of this constellation.

The placement of the Sun or Moon in the natal chart will show the directions taken, and of how Venus will spread her tentacles out to engulf the rest of the chart. In this chart, with this Capricorn Venus in the first house, it becomes much more physical in its needs than if it was in some other house. The direction that Venus searches for gratification will depend on whether it is the chart of a male, or female. In this case it is a male, and he only enjoys heterosexual relationships. To find the chosen direction of how Venus will react, we need to know where the Moon is placed in his chart.

We find it is in his third house. The aspect is a square to Venus so you know there is a constant source of energy from this aspect, good or bad. Now, adding another factor to the fire, the Moon is conjunct Uranus in the third house. What can happen with this kind of configuration? First, Venus the planet of love, and is involved from the first house, so it is a physical situation.
The aspect is a square, so this brings action, and the square to the Moon and with Uranus involved because of the conjunction.

To sum it up this person will become involved with women under unusual circumstance's, as the squared aspect will bring these encounters about. The first house of one's personality involved, and the third house of communication.

What takes place is a smooth talking man. One known for his charming ways. Because Venus is in Capricorn, and Capricorn is in a sense diplomatic. The sign of Capricorn also provides a good sense of humor, and women will like this in a man. This attraction makes the original bond even stronger.

The unusual circumstances come into play also because of the house position of the Moon. With the Moon representing women in his life, it can involve any connection to the third house. Yes it can involve relatives, and any female relative, no matter her connection to the family.

In chart 1A, when this boy's Point of Self reached seven years of age, he was introduced into the sexual world. A conjunction by age to the Moon, and a soft sextile aspect to Venus helped the introduction to be an enjoyable one.

The Sun Moon relationship is good and with Neptune in the eighth house, a strong sexual house, and it is trine to Venus. Consequently, the relationships with women throughout his life will be good. The two sisters living across the street brought a life's long lesson to this young boy. A lesson never forgotten.

Suppose it was a woman's chart and she had the same Venus in Capricorn configuration in the first house. This would have the same effect as chart 1A, if it was the Sun conjunct to Uranus in the third house,

What would happen to a woman with this configuration is that she would become involved with the males from within the family, or any male connected to the family, or from within the neighborhood.

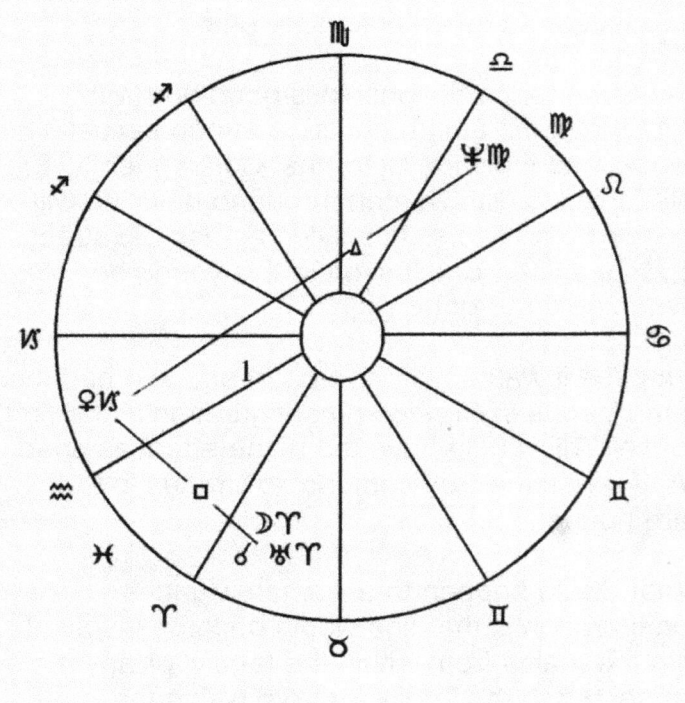

CHART 1A

CHART 2A

Using this woman's chart for a discussion we will go over some of the importance in learning life's lessons, and the ages at which they take place. In this case, the hard lesson was at the age of fourteen. The event was the rape of this child. The effects of this will cause her mental trauma for the rest of her life.

The point of self indicates the potential trauma at the age of fourteen, and was in an opposition to Neptune in the first house. Also, she was by age, square to Mars in the ninth house. Thus, the life long sexual attitude of the grown woman. The man, who took advantage of this young girl, came from the ninth house of theology. A man of the holy cloth. This is not to say that these events will take place in everyone's life, only that the potential always exists. You also have to take into consideration of how the person with any particular sun sign would behave in its normal manner, and as to how the relationship would start or stop.

There can be some potential problems caused when the Sun & Uranus are in conjunction in a woman's chart. Or, in the case of a man, it would be when the Moon & Uranus are in conjunction in their natal chart. As this is an indication of unusual conditions with the opposite sex.

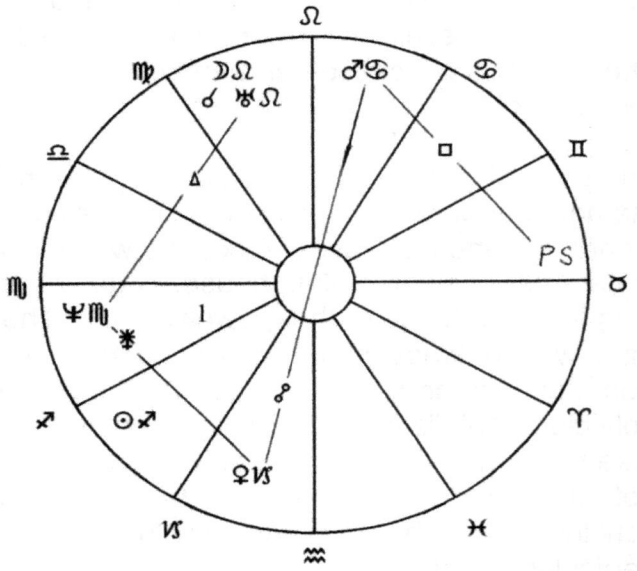

CHART 2A

ASPECTS OF INTEREST

Venus is of course, always involved in a person's love life, and from the very beginning of ones sexual interests, until the end of life. The constellation it is in at the time of birth will tell of its intensity in the individual's life.

Venus is not the only planet involved, as Neptune, Uranus, Pluto, Saturn, the Sun, Moon, and Mars need to be observed as well. The houses to consider are the first, third, seventh, eighth and the twelfth. Yet, there can be other houses involved.

As to how someone's love life starts out, good or bad, look to Neptune's influence. It is often in an aspect to either the Sun, or Moon in a chart, and it can have an aspect to the point of self in the beginning of the sexual enlightenment.

Quite often, the planet Neptune can be found in a square or an opposition aspect to the point of self. Because Neptune is the planet of deception, it may be the prime factor for a person's first love affair. It can also be the prime factor for the remainder of ones life. The question is, is Neptune allowing the individual to lie to themselves about their love life, or does it add a certain mystique to the unknown love they may be seeking at any time in their life.

The bad news part of the aspects, are the ones that involve the Venus curse, and that involve children. Though, this is not a topic I want to discuss, it is in reality, something that takes place. Perhaps the more important astrological planetary positions for a parent to watch, would be a child who has Neptune conjunct the first house cusp, or Neptune in the third house. If it is in the first house, odds are the passage of learning about sex, will be a safe passage.

If Neptune is in the third house, guard the child during the years of five to seven, as these can be potentially dangerous years. Not in every case, but it is better to be especially careful during these years. When the child has grown to adulthood, and when the Point of Self reaches an opposition to the third house Neptune, care should also be taken. If Neptune is in the sixth or twelfth house, it may be wise to see that the child is kept as safe as possible in the early teenage years. This is a time, when a young person considers the giving of himself or herself freely, but it is also a time of being taken without consent. There are other years of course, but the more important ones will fall about the age of twelve, to the age of seventeen.

The ages of five to seven have been discussed, as have the ages of twelve to fifteen. Yet, the ages in opposition to these ages should be considered as well. This would be ages of nineteen to twenty one, and the ages of twenty-six to twenty nine. When you find where your 'Point of Self' was located in your chart at the time of your original sexual encounter, the loss of your virginity, look to see when you will pass over that same location by age the second time. Such as having Neptune in the third house.

Let's say you were fifteen years old at the time. When you add twenty-eight years to that age, which would be the second time around, you will be forty-three years old. If the first time was an unhappy situation, it may be easier to move ahead in your life this time, forgetting the past, and perhaps a time of sexual enlightenment. If the first time was pleasant, the second time could be a time of much greater sexual enjoyments.

Uranus is always a planet of interest, especially if it is in a conjunction to either the Moon or Sun. If it is in conjunction to the Sun, the individual will have unusual relationships with men. If it is in conjunction to the Moon, the individual will have unusual relationships with women. The house it is in at the time of birth will tell you who might be involved. The problem with Uranus being involved in a conjunction with either luminary, the Sun or Moon, is that Uranus always wants a change. This can produce a constant struggle for the person who has this luminary aspect in their natal chart. The relationship they are currently in, may be the best they've ever had, yet Uranus always tugs at them to try someone new. There is no doubt that this can be an ongoing struggle.

It seems, that whenever the Point of self, by age, is in a conjunction, square, or opposition to the first house cusp, the sexual encounters can be harsh. This would be the ages of 7, 14, 21, 28, 35, 42, 49, 56, 63, 70, 77, and 84. Though not all of these ages may produce a sexual danger to someone, danger could present itself.

Neptune really is a planet of deception, when you consider that a youngster going through the sixth house by age, using the point of self, eleven years eight months, to fourteen years, is in reality going through an opposition to the twelfth house ruled by Neptune. I suggest you read the section referring to the light and dark parts of a chart.

Someone at the age of fourteen, and still in the dark part of the chart, will often wish others would notice them. This will be a youngster, who will try to delude others into thinking he, or she, is really someone from an older age group on the light side of the chart.

They may lie about their age, or do things someone older would do to convince this peer group, that they should be accepted as an equal. An act many of us have played when we were younger, but it can backfire.

If, as a child, you are accepted by an older peer group, especially if it is at your insistence, the consequences can be overwhelming. You may trigger your own introduction into the sexual world whether you are ready for it or not. All brought about because of a Neptune influence. This does not include a younger age group.

The house position can be any astrological house where children are involved. That is which house rules which kind of child. Your own children, stepchildren, cousins, grandchildren, etc.

Most marked events in our lives take place when the more prominent aspects are triggered. Such as sextiles, squares, trines and oppositions. Aspects are aspects, it matters not which ones are involved, each, has a separate effect that triggers some other portion of the chart. The aspects involved will trigger the outcome, as it does in any event.

This is one of those situations that brings the point home about the good or bad nature of aspects. Good aspects are often taken for granted yet they can lead to someone letting their guard down so to speak. The bad aspects could be used for self-defense instead of causing the outcome to be of a negative reaction. This is the main focus of using astrology as a tool, when you see the potential of a chart, you can be forewarned of danger, and hopefully made aware of a better path to travel in life.

QUARTER COMPOSITES & THE INDIVIDUAL

Quarter composites are determined by counting the house locations of the planets in a chart and are the strongest three houses in a chart. There is far more to quarter composites, than what will appear here, as the information furnished here is more in line with the theme of this book.

By using the Chart 1B, below, you can see there are six planets on the west side of the chart, and four on the east side, which makes the West side the strongest half section of the chart so far. Then you count again and you find there are six planets below the horizon on the south half, and four above in the north half. This makes the south half the strongest of these two halves.

Combining the two different, and stronger halves, you come up with the south west quarter as the strongest quarter composite for this chart, and it has been marked accordingly. Try doing this for your own natal chart to find your strongest quarter.

This chart is being used primarily for the purpose of explaining some item in this book, and in no way is it related to anyone this author knows.

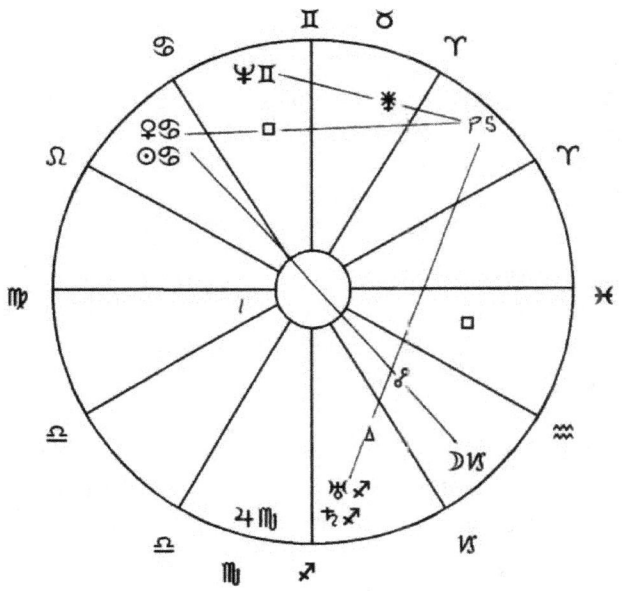

CHART 1B

FIRST QUARTER
HOUSES ONE, TWO and THREE, involve the following.

The first quarter is one of Impulses. Planets in this quarter do our subconscious bidding, and this is a quarter composite that provides us with survival instincts, and self-defense. It also has some influence on our procreation processes. In our early years, ages one through seven, it seems we may put more emphasis on self-substantiation and personal identification. As this is the period of self-consciousness, it is also a period of learning about ourselves bodily.

So what is it that this person does to attract events to themselves, and why? For one thing, the planets located in this lower part of the chart, on the dark side, that is below the elliptical plane, or horizon, are not seen by most others.

Thinking in this manner, a child that is taken advantage of while the 'Point of Self' is in this quarter, may not tell others of the abuse. Odds are the child will not fully understand that what has happened, nor why.

In some cases, such as in chart 1A, the boy who was introduced to sex at the age of seven by two sisters from his neighborhood, it may appear as though no harm was done. Chart 1A falls into this quarter composite, the incident led to a lifetime of fulfilling the unwritten promise of the two girls who lived across the street. The promise that others living close by, as in the neighborhood, or related, were open for fun and games.

The square from Venus in the first house of physical being, to the Moon and Uranus conjunction in the third house, can, and does continually cause problems.

SECOND QUARTER
HOUSES FOUR, FIVE and SIX, involve the following.

This section is mostly one of instincts. In all of my reference books, not one gives reference to the word, 'Incest,' though I feel it often starts in this quarter composite.

The child who experiences this kind of sexual abuse, will in some cases be held back in life. This holding back will be done mostly on a mental basis at the time. But, over a period of time, the child could be held back on a physical basis as well. It's highly possible, that this child may be restrained in some ways by their family influences until they are in their late thirties or forties. This, in the long run, affects their place in life. A good share of the time what they do in life will be directed by their family. Or, on what they feel they may owe the family, whether or not they really do owe the family anything.

Consider the planets Uranus, Neptune, Sun, or the Moon, and look to the fifth house. Though, the fourth house of home will play a part as well, and the sixth house can be involved.

THIRD QUARTER
HOUSES SEVEN, EIGHT, and NINE, involve the following.

This quarter is one of thinking, and a persons mentality. There are some downfalls to this quarter, but this is probably one of the safest sexual quarters in a birth chart.

This portion of the chart, is by age, the area where most people give of themselves freely to another as a lover. Such as charts 3A, 4A, and 5A. This is the kind of individual who is physically, and emotionally receptive, also mentally active, as well as outgoing.

This quarter is important because this person is trying to measure up to public opinion. It matters a great deal to this individual what other people think of them, and, they will guard their public image. They think this way, because these are planets in the light side of the chart, above the elliptical plane, or horizon, and nearest to the sunlight.

The chances this person takes, or experiences they have, often affects their marriage, or partnerships of any kind. As this quarter involves the seventh house, and is in opposition to the first house of themselves. With the eighth house involved, the end of relationships can take place.

FOURTH QUARTER
HOUSES TEN, ELEVEN, and TWELVE, involve the following.

This is a quarter of personal being. This is taking what comes along in life and dealing with it as needed. This is a quarter composite where you learn to take responsibility for yourself, and wanting to find your place in the world. This can also be a quarter where the person may chose seclusion. A part of life where this individual may live in a world, that to others, would think of as isolated.

Though, to look at chart 2B below, you would not expect this to be the case, as this person has all but Neptune above the horizon. This is a very public person, yet her quarter composite is the fourth quarter, the isolated world. Of course, it is a self-imposed isolation.

Yet, this quarter brings forth, outgoing people. People, who are not only active, they are emotional, physical, and often very mental. This, is someone who can become a very good poet, someone who pours out his or her inner feelings through the written word.

In chart 6A, the self-isolation, resulting from the beating and rape, of this young girl, will be overcome when her 'Point of Self' passes over Neptune again in her third house at the age of 34.

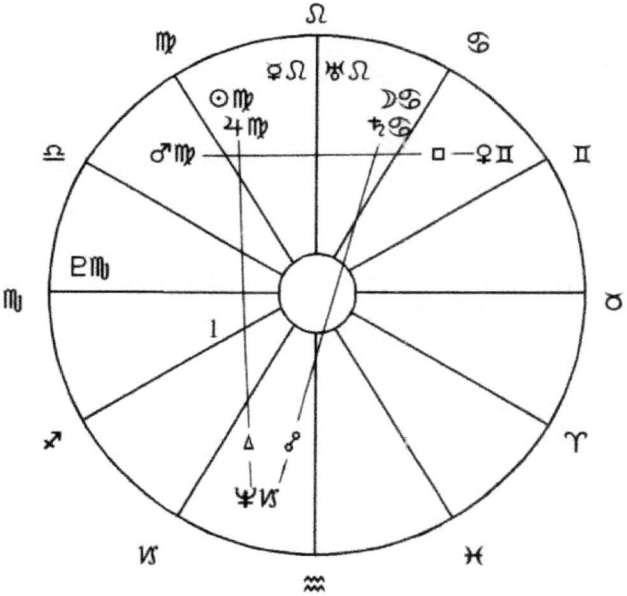

CHART 2B

THE LIGHT AND DARK PORTIONS OF A CHART

As the tenth house cusp represents 'Noon', and the seventh house cusp falls on six PM. Similarly, the fourth house cusp then becomes 'Midnight,' and the first house cusp is six AM.

When you think about a chart in this manner, you will understand that all of the planets falling between six AM and six PM are in the light part of the day. It seems that because these planets are above the horizon, or, elliptical plane, that others will notice these planetary conditions much easier than if they were on the dark side of the chart. Of course the planets between six PM and six AM are in the dark side of the chart, and go unseen by others. The closer to midnight, the harder they are to see.

As it happens, a chart with planets below the elliptical plane can get away with nearly anything, or everything, and will rarely get caught doing things considered wrong by others. Simply because the are in the darker part of the chart and will go un-observed. However, any planets at the top of the chart, will be very apparent to others.

To put this in perspective in your mind, think of it this way, you are in a well lit room, and looking through an open doorway into a room that is totally dark. You can't see very far into the dark room, and the farther in you look, the darker it gets. This would be the dark side of the chart.

Now, suppose you are standing in the far reaches of the dark room. You can easily see anything in the well-lit room beyond, as there is nothing to restrict your view. Though a few things might have shadows. In the center, and near the light, the mid-heaven, there aren't even shadows to interfere with your view.

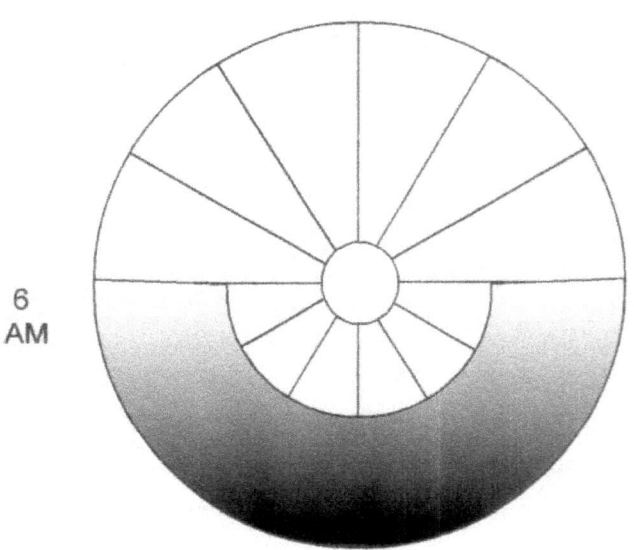

THE CYCLES OF MARRIAGE AND DIVORCE

There are many cycles in life, and many of those are of interest to lovers. A few are very important to married couples, or those considering marriage. You must remember there are ongoing events, such as marriages, divorces, and other life altering occurrences. The cycles presented here are indeed, surprising, and possible in any couples life together. The ideas presented here can be considered as curses when it becomes your turn to experience them.

The first statistical studies that produced an interest by this author, were published in the book 'Cycles, The Mysterious Forces that Trigger Events,' by Edward R. Dewey, and copyrighted in 1971. Over the years, this author's own research has verified these findings, and more.

Having read this book in 1971, and having since read several other writings on cycles, I made it a point to ask very personal questions of people in regards to their individual, and marital well being. All questions were asked without discrimination as to the sex of the individual, and these questions were directed at both, people going through happy and difficult times in their lives. The intention was to obtain the details needed. Much of which you will find written here. Perhaps, to satisfy your own interests.

MARRIAGE.
Perhaps you've just met someone who has sparked your passionate, and intimate feelings. The chemistry of love takes control of your life, and all reason goes right out the window. Perhaps the chemistry lies. The wanting of another person in our lives can lead us down the wrong path in seeking the correct mate. This often happens even when we have a mate, or commitment to someone currently in our lives. The problem encountered by most people is that they attempt to make themselves a couple with someone they have chosen, and perhaps, even when their own personal love life needs do not match the other persons correctly.

With married couples, when one of the harder cycles takes place, its affect is to end a seemingly sound marriage. Most of this takes place at a time when the couples are well established. Financially, and domestically. A time that you, as an observer, would think all is well, and it may have been.

This particular cycle interrupts a marriage, often ending it, when it reaches the mature age of 18.2 years. There are many marriages that end before, and after this time frame, but this cycle is consistent, and ongoing. There are several contributing factors, a few of which may pique your interest are discussed here.

In a sense, you would think the 18.2 year marital cycle would involve all marital age groups, but it does not. When you consider that one of the first age groups to suffer stressful times, regarding marriage, or seemingly solid relationships, is less than thirty years of age. An age factor that would require the couple to have started the relationship at the age of twelve.

The reasons for the divorce are usually caused by circumstances brought on by sexual infidelities, or incompatibilities due to mental growth. These are not the only reasons, money is a close runner up. The best possibility for a successful marriage the first time, is when the two people are over the age of twenty. At least the age of twenty for women and the age of twenty-three or four for men is best. Men much younger than this are, as a rule, just not ready for the marital commitment. Often it is simply because they are not mature enough. A better age would be after the 'Point of Self' passes over the Mid-heaven, and enters the tenth house.

DIVORCES

It is not unusual for two people to spend year after frustrated year with the wrong mate. Sometimes you will come across an older couple who just seem to live with each other, and they may just barely get along with one another. The constant bickering that takes place between them daily places their family in awkward positions. Even their children do not want to be around them because of the stress. Did they choose the wrong mate when they were younger, then stay together for the sake of the children? You know it happens, but what a shame. It could have been avoided by making a better choice in the beginning.

The more noticeable age cycle, for individuals to become divorced, is on average, 29.45 years. Friction in marriages for this age group starts when the individuals are about 26 years old. By the time they are age 28, they know many of the problems in their lives are being fueled, not only by themselves, but also by their marital, or sometimes non-marital mates.

By the age of 29, the destiny of a Uranus and Saturn involvement will again bring their planetary powers to bear on this age group. A curse, well the results often leave one or both ex-partners cursing.

One, or the other, of the marital partnership, will pull the plug on the relationship and seek a divorce, or an ending to the relationship. This particular age group often wants their freedom so badly, they seem to work against themselves in obtaining their freedom. When this happens they place themselves in another seven-year cycle. This next seven year cycle period involves personal struggles. After a parting of the ways has taken place, the two individuals now need to maintain two separate homes, and still be able to communicate with the ex-spouses family if children are involved.

TURNING THE CORNER

It may seem as though you will never be rid of the ongoing problems you encounter. First it's as if you are completely alone in the world, then you find you can't make ends meet as your money just doesn't come in as fast as it goes out. There is however, a positive life cycle starts about 35 years of age. This takes place after the six to seven year struggle period that came into your life about of the 29.45 year divorce cycle, and Saturn has been playing a heavy role in this part of your life.

At this time the resistance from the past, and the struggles, will begin to fade away. This is turning the corner for many people, and a continuous upward spiral of better things to come. Well, almost. There is one more cycle to upset a few marriages, we know about this part of life, we call it the Mid-life crisis.

MID-LIFE CRISIS

In a sense you would think the 18.2 year marital cycle would be the end of this kind of stressful nonsense, but it isn't. It has been found that the next contributing demise to marriages is when one partner, or the other, enters what we've come to call, the mid-life crisis of life.

The Point of Self will be found in the seventh house at this time. At a point in a person's age, which seems as if it might be too late to make major changes in one's life style. You've heard them say, "I've just got to find myself." Isn't it interesting to note that this generally falls about the age of 42-44?

It's as if we are working against ourselves, and against our own families. It seems as if it is a time for that fancy new sports car, and perhaps someone new has entered our lives, someone who catches our fancy and makes us feel younger than we really are.

In reality, this is nearly what happens to each of us, yet it is slightly different for both the male, and female. In many cases, the ages may run from 42 to 46, more, or less.

The male of our species is, at this age, trying to maintain his virility, and his ability to attract women, especially women younger than himself. It seems a last chance at being a competing male.

At the same time, he wants to keep what he has worked all his life to attain. Still he takes the chance, possibly throwing it all away for one last fling at life. Often a costly fling.

The female however, is just now reaching a point in her life where she is experiencing her greatest sexual fulfillment. This is a time when she has cast away the inhibitions from earlier years. Now she finds out she can really enjoy a sexual encounter. She puts her all into the relationship, and may even devour a man who has thought of her as timid, or withdrawn.

THE LAST CHANCE

For those of us, who may have not made the change for the better, at the age of 29 years, the age of 56 seems to be the last chance to rid ourselves of a bad relationship. One last chance to start anew. This is not a cycle seen often, but it does take place when the Point of Self transits the first house for the second time.

LOOKING AGAIN

A contributing factor to many of these problems is another cycle we hear little about. This is a curse of mankind in general; male of female it does not matter. It is a cycle that interferes with our lives, though it may be one of the unconscious mind. Its influence is one that brings many unhappy situations to bear. It does not seem to matter that you may have a mate already, it's nature's way.

If you are single, this cycle may not have a profound impact on your life, as this cycle is one that takes place every 7 or 8 years. That is, the looking for a new mate.

YOUR MARITAL BLISS, OR IS IT?

Why is it some marriages are alive, and very healthy, while others die miserably? Often the reasons are quite simple; it is a matter of understanding where you are in your life. To some folks this may seem a foreign thought, but the outcome of your marriage may depend on where you and your mate are in your individual life cycles.

You, as the reader, need to read the whole book to decide who you really are, and what Sun sign might be best for you. Honesty is crucial, and though some of the Sun signs sound like an exciting possibility to you, take care, it might be a good time at your expense. None of the Sun signs are perfect, though many of them will think they are.

There are a few lucky people who seem to find a life's soul mate for life. We see them in supermarkets, on the sidewalks, in the parks, they are the couple holding hands as they walk along. It's not a put on, it's real. It is easy to see they are walking life's path together. Where you find one, you find the other, it's a never wanting to be apart. Most just seem to have Been lucky, but it's the wise person who chooses their mate carefully.

This next section deals with each of the Sun signs, and their potential ability to marry successfully. At the same time, the information presented here will tell of some of the negative factors to be found.

These are written with the most favorable signs first, and descending in order of strength. You may not agree with the chosen order in which they are written, and though it is only my opinion, it is very close to the truth.

CANCER

This is the natural homemaker. Someone who feels the need to have a home life, and will work hard at making it come true. This is a very romantically, imaginative, and emotional person. When it comes to their love life, this is one of the more faithful Sun signs. Even though this is the natural homemaker, they can miss the true love boat until later in life.

Some of the problems with having this Sun sign as your mate are as follows.

A negative side would be the possibility of continual nagging, a common event with this sign. They are highly emotional and cannot take criticism. If you offer constant criticism to this mate, the marriage will fail. If the marriage begins to fail, the Cancer Sun sign may become greedy, holding onto everything, and everyone. The point is, can the marital mate handle it.

You have never experienced a bad temper, until, you are set upon by an angry Cancer Sun sign. You cannot escape the crushing crabs claw, and they know if anger does not work, tears will.

However, if this is your mate, expect him, or her to work at keeping the relationship together. It matters not whether it is good for either of you.

TAURUS

This person needs the solidity of a good marriage, and that of a good home life. The solidity of marriage shows others that this person is successful at any undertaking, and their self-determination will fight to keep the marriage together.

The Taurus is a highly sexually stimulated sign. To the physical extent, that many mates may not last long enough to take care of this individual's needs, and this is in the normal sexual relationship. If, their needs include something outside the normal realm, it can be even harder to cope with.

Some of the problems with having this Sun sign as your mate, are as follows.
If the marriage goes belly up, how do you shed yourself of this mate? You may not be able too without some real effort on your Part. Remember you are a possession to this Sun sign, perhaps even after the divorce is final.

Do you want to be possessed, if not stay away from this Sun sign. It will seem as if they own their mates, and their children. They accept anything being offered, physical, or mental, but don't expect to get anything in return. Remember this is the person who is materialistic in every sense.

CAPRICORN

This Sun sign may be too busy to stray from the marital bed, in fact perhaps too busy to spend much time in it with the chosen spouse either. This is the politician, no matter what the platform may be. The Sun sign of Capricorn is not known as a lustful sign, but Venus in this sign is another matter. This person can talk to the opposite sex, about sex, with little self-consciousness; it is after all, a topic of mutual interest.

Some of the problems with having this Sun sign as your mate are as follows.

Be careful in choosing this sigh as your mate, be sure what they prefer, man or woman. When in a good marriage with a Capricorn, if you stray from the marital bed it will not be forgotten, or forgiven. Never mind they may also stray.

This Sun sign may be too busy to get things done for you, and perhaps they may seem to be a cold person. The sense of humor is inviting, but it invites everyone. Often, their invitation includes you letting them come into the privacy of your home. Or, was that the bedroom.

SCORPIO

They say this sign is a highly sexual oriented sign, perhaps, but don't depend on it. Yet, if you are one of those chosen by this Sun sign as a mate, expect them to be with you through thick or thin. In fact this person may be with you even if the marriage is over with, they just don't realize its finished.

Some of the problems with having this Sun sign as your mate, are as follows.

You will never have a secret from this person. Somehow, they will find out anything they want to know, and they want to know everything about you, or anyone connected with you, and everyone else for that matter.

This Sun sign is similar to that of Taurus, in that it is possessive. If the marriage goes on the rocks, this person does not want to give it up. If you wrong this Sun sign while married, you will come to understand the word, 'revenge.' Oh, you may not be divorced, but you will wish you were. You will suffer, even if it is done quietly.

Did this person marry you for your money, are you sure? Were you aware of their jealous streak before you married.

VIRGO

If, you are chosen by this Sun sign as a life's mate, odds are you really are in it for the long haul. As this Sun sign rarely marries until they are sure they have chosen wisely. This is not someone to jump into marriage hastily. This may not be an overly exciting sign, but they will be a very faithful mate.

Some of the problems with having this Sun sign as your mate, are as follows.

Do not expect this to be a doting parent, children can get on a Virgo Sun signs nerves. Children can just be too untidy, too messy, or too noisy, etc. You may wonder why they have children when they want to just put them in a corner somewhere.

If your marital position is deteriorating while you are married to a Virgoan, do not think it will be an easy path to travel. It won't be. This person can make your life a living hell. You've never heard real criticisms until you are on the bad side of this Sun sign. You will hear complaints that you never realized needed attention until you begin having problems while married to a Virgo.

Before you agree to wed this sign, be sure you understand their sexual desires, and the gender they prefer.

AQUARIUS

This can be a choosy marital partner, if this is your mate, it may have taken him or her, awhile for them to find you. The wise ones do not rush into marriage. They don't rush because they are too choosy. Once married to the correct mate, it will be a rare Aquarian to wander from the marital bed. This may be because they are often very busy taking care of the world.

Some of the problems with having this Sun sign as your mate, are as follows.

This Sun sign doesn't like to work, that is why there are more inventors from this sign than any of the other signs. They invent things so they won't have to work so hard.

It goes without question that this is a humanitarian. This person will be so busy doing good, that his or her own family may lack some of this caring attitude at home. Can they make mistakes, of course not, just ask one of them. Well, none that they will admit to if they have some planets in Virgo.

The male of this Sun sign, may have a wandering eye for the opposite sex. Though he may not have the tendency to having an indiscreet affair, he will. He would rather, if possible, make it a legal joining.

LEO

As the ruler of the house of love, Leo falls in love easily. Not necessarily wisely, or fortunately, but easily. It is by natures wish that the Sun sign Leo should be joined with a mate, and this Sun sign dislikes being alone. They want someone to shine for, and, as a result, they often place their mates on pedestals. Though it can devastate them when their chosen mate actually falls off the pedestal, and becomes a regular human being. You know, someone with faults.

Some of the problems with having this Sun sign as your mate, are as follows.

As the mate to this sign you will not mind getting the gifts. The Leo Sun sign bestows gifts to those they fancy. However, will you, as their mate, put up with the gift giving to others.

If you are deeply involved with a Leo sun sign, you will need to constantly bolster this person's ego, it is expected of you. Will you love them, no question, at least until it ends.

PISCES

It may seem as if they will marry any Sun sign, and they might, but it is a necessity for this Sun sign to marry correctly to attain marital bliss. They need someone who understands their sensitivities; their day dreaming of better things. They build castles in the air, as they have a pie in the sky attitude. To those who wed this Sun sign, just being a Pisces can be a curse, as their emotional state can be a senseless well of endless emotions. This Sun sign is probably the most charitable sign of all.

Some of the problems with having this Sun sign as your mate, are as follows.

This can be a problem drinker, or a user of drugs. This can lead to several problems, perhaps often straying from the marital bed, not to mention the addictions. If they have Venus in Aquarius, you'll have to take care of their bedroom needs as well.

This is someone similar to that of the Cancer, or Scorpio Sun signs, in the sense that they will seem to be suffering in some manner. They can suffer from anything they want when it the excuse is needed. You may never know what it will be that they suffer from, how can you possibly know, they don't know either. Cancer will cry, Scorpio will blame you, but Pisces does not know who's at fault.

LIBRA

The problem of making up their mind extends into the marital relationship as well. This Sun sign takes a long time to choose a mate, so long that most of us would tire of the extended search. Because of their idealistic feelings about marriage, theirs should last. They have little interest in different partners. This is not a Sun sign to create waves in their lives, they don't want to face the aftermath caused by problems anyone creates. They tend to see the world through rose colored glasses.

Some of the problems with having this Sun sign as your mate, are as follows.

You may find yourself making many of the decisions for this person, well maybe not all of them, but at least the important ones. And get used to having others do stuff for them, even if you would have gotten around to it, it is their nature to have others do things for them. No, they won't have to ask, it will be just be understood.

GEMINI

Even if they don't think so, this is a Sun sign that needs to be married. This is a mind that constantly needs nourishment, even if the children need help with their homework, this one has their own studies to deal with. Sexual enjoyment will come after the mental studies have taken place.

Yet, this is a continual student, some think of Gemini as a cold Sun sign. The mind does not seem to shut down long enough to enjoy a sexual encounter. Anyone, who seems slow, may be an irritation to this person, to the point that they may even become cranky and quite annoyed with those close to them. Okay, maybe anybody close by.

Some of the problems with having this Sun sign as your mate, are as follows.

This Sun sign is similar, in a sense, to that of a Scorpio. This sign may make more out of a conversation than is really there. It's as if they think there is something written between the lines that does not exist.

There is no sense in giving this person hell for making a mistake, as they themselves don't have any idea how it happened.

You must keep this Sun sign busy in a marriage. If not, they will become bored, and you don't want a bored mate who seeks a new experience. Does this mate of yours seem to travel a great deal, perhaps gone for days at a time, you might want to consider that perhaps there is another family with the same last name as your own living somewhere along the traveled path.

If you are contemplating a divorce from Gemini, watch out for the checks written on your bank account. Did you really write them, or were they written for you, and of course your signature appears on the checks.

ARIES

This, is someone who lives for a danger of some sort. Though they don't think their currently chosen path is really all that dangerous, you, or I, wouldn't try doing the same thing. This is an easier sign for men than for women. The men need a weaker mate who is satisfied to remain in the background. An Aries woman is often too strong for most men, yet she needs a strong mate. Not a mate to rule her, well not all of the time anyway, but a mate who can stand up to her, and hold his own.

Some of the problems with having this Sun sign as your mate, are as follows.

This is someone who can fall in love quickly, and they fall out just as quickly. They may show a jealous streak you didn't know was there before you married them, but you will find out if the Aries thinks you are getting too chummy with anyone else. Had they been married before you came along, odds are they were. Odds are they will be married again after you have left their marital bed.

SAGITTARIUS

This is not someone who likens to marriage easily, its like putting ice cream into a hot oven and expecting it to stay frozen, it will not happen. Once married, it will be an unusual event for the Sagittarian to stray from the marital bed. Oh, it can happen, but they will be concerned with what others think of them, which may be what keeps them on the straight and narrow.

A Sagittarian is a poor liar, but they can spot one easily, and if you think this is an un-educated person, think again.

Some of the problems with having this Sun sign as your mate, are as follows.

This is someone who needs to be free. Though they do marry, they are at a constant battle with the opposite sex. This is a Sun sign that can wander from bed to bed if their mate is of a narrow mind, or restrictive. They may do this just to see if they can win the game. They will try to get away with nearly everything they do that seems to be wrong by the rest of us, and most of the time they do.

SUN, MOON, AND ASCENDING SIGN COMBINATIONS

Any chart indicating someone who has the Sun, Moon, and Ascending sign in the same constellation, is a person to be reckoned with. Especially if the Sun and Moon are withing a few degrees of the cusp. The last twenty degrees of the twelfth house and the first ten degrees of the first house, is a power area. These particular planets involve the individuality, the personality and the emotional mentality. Though this is not the same as a stellium, it is a strong indication of how this individual will react to anything in life.

When you meet someone who has any double sign, that is Sun and Moon, or a triple combination in the same sign, Sun, Moon, and ascending sign, beware.

I am not saying they will be bad for you, but you need to do your homework before you make a final decision as to this combination as a mate. Be certain, you understand what it is you are letting yourself in for. This, is a blending of planets that you want to understand before you take on the power this combination can amass.

STELLIUMS

Stelliums are considered, in general, to have at least five planets in one sign at the time of birth. These are not as unusual as it might seem. When a person has as little as, three or four planets in one sign, perhaps just the Sun, Moon, and ascending sign in one constellation, it has an impact on the persons life.

Stelliums can be tough on the individual, though they won't know this about themselves until the rest of us tell them, *"You're weird."* A stellium can easily overshadow the natural Sun sign when it occurs in a sign other than the birth sign constellation.

People with stelliums do not realize how narrow-minded they may be in their beliefs, but how can they know, when they have nothing with which to compare their lives. Those of us who do not have these planetary conditions placed upon us, may realize the problems the other person is suffering with. There are many, many planetary configurations with three or four planets in the same constellation, but they are so numerous that there will not be any of those listed in this book. Stelliums can be difficult to deal with in your life, but they can become easier to live with, if the individual understands what influences the stellium has in their life.

The affects on a person will be increased with each additional planet in a stellium at the time of their birth. We will not go into great depth on the discussion of stelliums.

When considering how a stellium affects you, always be sure to use the ones that include the Sun, and Moon. You will find there are times when there are stelliums of five planets in the same constellation that include the other planets, but the ones with the most power will include the luminaries. The Sun and Moon should be included because this is a huge part of a person's individuality. Of course Mercury should be included as it rules the manner of thinking or learning. Also, because it is always close to the Sun.

You will find that they take place about twice a year, sometimes only once. It is interesting to note that one of the greatest stelliums to take place in recent history happened in February of 1962, when seven planets were in the sign of Aquarius. The Sun, Moon, Mercury, Venus, Mars, Jupiter, and Saturn.

With the power of seven planets in the sign of Aquarius, these people will sway the way world's thinking and the direction of our future. You will not find these people thinking of the here and now, as today is much to close a time frame.

They have already done their contemplative thinking on this time frame, their minds are way ahead of the remainder of our collective thinking. Will they make changes in the daily lives of the worlds population, you can count on it, and the changes will be very different than what we as a people might expect. Once they start taking positions of power, the world will never be the same again. Will it be a better place, you can bet it will.

THE STRUGGLE YEARS

On average, there are three potential struggle times in our lives, and each of us goes through them. Some get through these trying times easier than others. The toughest of the three periods is the first one, and it is the toughest because the planet Saturn is very involved, as is the planet Uranus.

These struggle cycles are easy to follow if you consider where the Point of Self is by age. If you do not understand the *'Point of self'*, read that section in this book, to make this part of the book more easily understood. Basically, it is where you are by age in your life on an astrological basis.

These struggle periods take place as you pass, by age, through the first, second and third houses. The first house represents you as an individual, and your physical being. The second house involves your monetary well being, and the third house brings new developments into your living conditions, or your living sphere. Communications play a large part in this passage through the third house. Then when you enter the fourth house, it is as if turning the corner to better times. Read the section about 'Turning the Corner' in the section, 'The cycles of Marriage and Divorce.'

THE FIRST STRUGGLE PERIOD

The indication of the struggles to come, can actually start a year or two ahead of the time where the decisions have to be made. These are decisions in regards to changes in your lifestyle. It is the possibility of a major decision, we are going to discuss here.

In the point of self-theory, the first house cusp is where it all begins, and this is the cusp where you start counting. You allow two years and four months per house. It takes twenty-eight years for the Point Of Self to complete one journey around the natal chart. When you reach the age of twenty-eight, you are back at the beginning, so to speak.

Just prior to returning to the first house cusp, your life has been passing through the twelfth house. The twelfth house is a restrictive house, so tensions in your life may have been building slowly. At the age of twenty-eight, you find you are at a crossroads in life.

Each time you return to the first house, in this twenty-eight cycle, a need for a change in your life will start. It is the influence of Uranus that will bring this need for change into your life. In a sense, Uranus promotes rebellion, and odds are the changes have not have been planned.

You may even think you can put up with the existing conditions in your life. However, at the age of twenty-nine, plus a few months, the planet Saturn returns to its natal location. As Saturn does the subconscious bidding in your life, its influence will be to shed the problems, and to move ahead in your life.

The problem you need to get rid of can come from any corner of your life, but most of the time it is a personal relationship. This is a time, when young couples decide to go their own separate ways, and it is hardest on young mothers who find themselves on their own, most of them will be raising children.

From the age of twenty-eight, to thirty years four months, it is a very personal struggle. Perhaps even to the point of wondering if it is worth the struggle. From the age of thirty years four months, to thirty-two years eight months, it becomes more of a financial struggle. The trying to make ends meet on a salary that is far from adequate. A time where children need to have a mother, or a father, at home, and often when a parent cannot be there for them.

From the age of thirty-two years eight months, to thirty-five years of age, the harder struggles begin to diminish, or soften in their influence. You may have moved to a new neighborhood, or you may be making new friends who are making things easier.

The children's ages can help in making their management easier now, and at the age of thirty-five, a fourteen year rise to better things starts to take place.

THE SECOND STRUGGLE PERIOD
The second time through theses struggle periods, will be from the ages of fifty-six, to sixty-three. There are those who will demand of themselves that they get through the first hard decision at twenty nine years of age, with the intention of keeping the relationship intact. If they manage to work through the hardships, and a few do, this second time through these three houses, is the time that the decision must be faced once and for all. Just the getting through the years between the first time through these houses and this time would have been very trying. Feeling for those you've been trying to keep a relationship with, may be, hateful.

The mental hassle of putting up with the unhappy conditions until now, can put that those same people into the hospital about the age of fifty-four, to fifty-six. As unhappy conditions can take a toll on one's health.

If the correct decision was made in the earlier years, this can be a good time for new beginnings. The new changes coming now, will not involve the planet Saturn like it did the first time. Now it is just the effects of Uranus. This planet will lead the decision maker into thinking ahead, 'what about my future.'

The second time through these houses, is the time to think about what kind of money will you need to retire on, or how high of a status do you think you need to live with, and to maintain. Now perhaps reality sets in, and you realize you do not have to live up to a high social standard anyway.

This is a time to get rid of old debts, because now you need to conserve your finances for the years to come.

Perhaps moving to a smaller home is best, and in a cheaper section of town, or even another area of the country. After all who do you have to impress, all of the others you have been struggling to out do, are cutting back on their expenditures as well. The children are gone, you don't really need that large home. Yet, there will be those of you who figure that a four or five bedroom house will be good for when the grandchildren come home to visit. You'll find out, that when they do come, it will be one or two at a time. Yes, the smaller two or three bedroom home would have been just fine.

THE THIRD STRUGGLE PERIOD

This comes about at the age of eighty four years. You would think the struggles would be over by now wouldn't you? Well, for most of us, it is.

Those who make it this far are again being faced with decisions to be made. Do you continue to live alone in some remote place, or do you move closer to the children. Are you financially able to continue on your own, should you be living in a retirement home, is your health good enough to let you maintain your independence, are you still able to drive your own car, and on and on it goes.

Surprising, as it seems, there are those who will make some major changes in their lifestyles even at this advanced age. Perhaps, something they have always wanted to do in their lives.

THE SEXUAL OUTLOOK

These are the basic sexual outlooks of the twelve constellations. This does not mean that when you talk to any one of these sun signs, that this information is ironclad. The reason for this statement is to make you, the reader, understand that there is far more to a sun sign's love life than this information. The aspects from one planet to the next, can, and often do, upset these basics. Remember this data is concerned only with the sun signs, if you consider the potential influences from their ascending signs as well, you can have another twelve directions to explore. Then of course there are the other planets in the individual's chart, Aspects of course, and . . . well you can see, it can vary greatly from person yo person.

THE ARIES MALE

This guy may be as tough as he looks. He is often well built physically, and he rarely backs away from a confrontation. He may also be very hard to deal with in any business situation, but in reality, he really wants a true and romantic love life.

As a young lover he lacks the knowledge, but is eager to learn the role of a lover. Once he learns, his sexual appetite can be insatiable. This lover may not be satisfied with one sexual encounter at a time; he may keep you in bed for several sessions of love making. Once this lover decides which mate he wants, male or female, the pursuit will end in conquest. Aries has a continuos drive for new experiences.

A problem this sun sign may encounter, will be one of a personal nature. His manner of dressing may not impress those he seeks. He needs to take care in his personal hygiene, such as shaving twice a day if needed. He needs to have bathed, and changed into fresh clothing before he attempts to contact someone he wants as a mate.

This is the guy who will make a sexual advance at the office, or anywhere for that matter. At parties, this male can tend to drink too much, and their moral etiquette can slip dramatically. This of course most often backfires on them and causes hard feelings among those concerned.

As a mate he can be very generous, perhaps without even thinking about it, but he can also be very jealous and demanding of his mate. The Aries male may not find true happiness until his later years. This would be after he outgrows the problem of being an impetuous lover in his early life. He needs to learn to enjoy what he has, and to live with it as long as he can. When it ends, he will be heartbroken, and you should be careful of his anger should it arise.

THE ARIES FEMALE

When this female finds out about sex, and this often happens at an early age, she is going to love the discovery. This woman can be a student of making love. She will know all about the physical body, his and hers.

Where another sun sign may want to read literature, this woman wants to read pornography. Look in her dresser drawers, if you dare, and you may find some interesting photographs. As this woman's lover, she likes a hands on man. Touching, feeling, patting her on the butt, and doing so anywhere at any time. Well, you get the idea. Like the Aries male, she has a continuos drive for new experiences.

A problem for this sun sign, is that she needs to be realistic with her men. She has a tendency to make them more than they really are in life. She can be overwhelmed by compliments, and they may seem extravagant to her, but she will take them. If her impatience with a lover takes hold, she can find a new lover nearly anywhere.

This woman can collect lovers continually, and she often starts at a young age. The men in her life may not understand her; this is not a dumbbell by any means, yet she has trouble finding men who are strong enough to take care of her needs.

She can devour a weak man quickly. In the long run, this becomes a problem because she needs a strong male in her life, but it may be her unconscious desire is to overwhelm men in general.

When men meet this woman, they know instinctively she is every bit a woman, still their egos make them charge full ahead into a relationship which they think they will control. Wrong again.

As a man in this woman's life, do not forget a birthday, or an anniversary, or any other dates that may seem important to her. You'll only do this once, maybe twice, and if you do, it will cost you.

You've heard the saying, 'The woman behind the man.' Well this is the woman.

THE TAURUS MALE

His sexual urges may make him a wealthy man. Primarily because he is of the opinion that money can buy anything. With a high libidinal mental energy, and preconceived attitudes in mind, he will work long and hard to acquire wealth. This is the man women like, because he wants to hear all about the woman he is with. He will urge them to talk to him, to tell him all about themselves. Should this approach fail, the listener will find him very talkative.

He looks for love conquests everywhere he goes, and when he finds them, he can be a very good lover. He is however, concerned with his needs first, then those of his lover, and finally the family. No, these individuals do not have to be part of the same group, that is lover and family. This man may make a play for another woman, no matter that one of his children, or even his current mate is with him at the moment.

This is very much a heterosexual man, and he looks forward to a sexually long and fulfilling life. As a young male, who is trying to discover his abilities, he will seek any easy prey. Those that seem easiest to catch. Sometimes it can involve an act of aggression.

THE TAURUS FEMALE

This can be too much of a woman for many men, as she can easily outlast most men. If they can't match her sexual appetite, she'll toss them away, but not before taking some kind of pleasure from them. This is not saying the men will enjoy it, but she will. This woman will find several variations of sex interesting, but what she wants is a man who can last for hours.

This can be the woman who has read every love manual available, studied every position, and knows how to keep her lover in check until she is ready to fulfill her own desirable finish. Any kind of lovemaking will be understood by this lover, and her male counterpart may not want to escape from her needs. Though once she has had a great lover, she may continue to look for the next perfect male, and she may not find him any to soon.

To better understand this woman and her love desires, look inside her closets, and dresser drawers. Don't move anything around, such as the handcuffs, the soft rope, the dildo, and don't mention you know she has them. Unless, of course, you want to become one of the toys. The way her bedroom is furnished may tell you a great deal. This woman likes luxury and comfort in all of her surroundings.

This woman, will look like a woman, the femininity will just ooze out of her. She will make it a point to look beautiful just for the sake of beauty, not necessarily to attract men. Though, they will no doubt notice her, as her natural being will demand their attention.

With women, there are two signs of the Zodiac that have big breasts, this one, Taurus, and the other is Cancer. This is not to say they will all have big breasts, but, if they are big, these are the signs that will have them. Other signs that have big breasts will most often have one of these two signs as an ascending sign. This being the first house cusp, and ruling the physical body.

This is someone who could care less one way or the other about becoming a mother. But when she does, she will prefer raising daughters if she has children at all. She will also be very protective of her children.

THE GEMINI MALE

This is another heterosexual male, in fact, perhaps more so than any other Sun sign. If there is to be an early marriage, this man may be the first among them. For a woman, to get this man in bed with her, will not be an easy task. Especially if she is of the same social standing, or peer group. Yet, if he is away from his home environment, he may try anything regarding romance and sex.

At home, he wants the traditional trimmings. Good clothing, accepted music, good art, traditional foods, and normal literature. Even the woman in his life must be conventional, and conservative. He will expect her to keep his house like his mother did, even if his mother didn't keep house.

If, as a woman, you want a really wild time in bed, odds are you won't find it with this man. His ideal woman will be his own age, and mild. Anything that seems erotic, may be outside his normal line of thinking.

THE GEMINI FEMALE

This woman is interested in sex, but only because as a woman, she knows it is going to happen at some point in her life. Often she will hold anything sexual at arm's length for as long as possible. Yet, if you are a woman, you couldn't ask for a better friend, than the Gemini woman.

Anything that resembles an out of ordinary sexual encounter can upset her. She will have no part in it, and the man in her life must be clean and neat, perhaps even with an effeminate way about him.

This is a person who will not rush into marriage, and she may put it off for some time while she makes the final decision. The decision will encompass not only the man she is considering, but his qualifications and ability as a lover. Then there is the question of whether she even wants to get married. .

Often she may put the marital factor off until later in her life. She will marry, because she knows it is an accepted way of life. Another reason for a late marriage, is the potential of having children. No sense in rushing into this field of danger.

There is another side to this woman, she can have an innate knowledge of how to bring a man to a state of excitement that few of the other signs can imagine. If it is only one night of love making, and she has taken care of her own needs, she may not even remember who he was.

Another side of her nature is interesting, she can outlast most men in bed. Even to the extent of saying things to him in the bedroom, that may surprise him. This can come about as part of her duality. She can be one woman in the bedroom, and quite another woman in the rest of the house. She may also start to experience the sexual part of life early, and may start a family early as well.

THE CANCER MALE

This is not a man who makes advances to women often, it's because he is afraid of rejection and will not subject himself to the potential torment. If he feels the woman of his choosing does not want him as he wants her, he feels he might as well take a cold shower. Though in reality this does little good. When he does find the right mate there will be a lot of noise coming from the bedroom. His, and hers.

If given encouragement this man can be a good lover, and a good mate. Ridicule him and he will hide himself as an Ostrich might bury its head in the sand. As the sign of Cancer the crab, you will find this man sidesteps issues that are un-settling to him. Often answering questions with questions.

This is the romantic male; he enjoys sex and lots of it, perhaps having sex with many different mates, as he may consider it as gaining experience. Part of this attitude can rub off in his marriage, as he may have his way with his mate, and once he is satisfied, he may no longer worry about her needs.

As he ages, the women he chooses to share in his life may get younger; it will not matter that others think him unwise.

This man is also a homebody. He wants a home a family, and a place of refuge from the world outside.

THE CANCER FEMALE

This is the feminine woman, and you can see this about her at any time. She will look feminine without trying too. This is also the natural mother, the homemaker, and when it comes to moods, she'll have those too. She will remember every anniversary, every birthday, or any special occasion involving the family.

If she becomes frustrated, and she will, she can escape the situation by eating or drinking. However, this is the drunk you don't want to be around. Her tears and her problems become open for discussion, and for your help. The problems she has can easily climb beyond your mental endurance. This is a woman who requires a protective mate; at least it will seem so. Be careful not to criticize this woman, if you do, beware her tongue lashing, it will sting as if you have stepped into a patch of nettles.

She likes older people, and the attention of older men. She discovers sex early in her life, and may experiment. If she is one to experiment, she will become a woman while still living in a girl's body. Though she is attracted to older men, she may try out a younger male just for the fun.

It is not unheard of for this fair maiden to retain her virginity until she is married. Even as a married woman, if problems arise in the marriage, she can easily find a lover who will appreciate her, and her body.

On the positive side, this is a person who wants to dedicate herself to motherhood, and that of a housewife. She wants to collect antiques, and have children. And, she wants to be happy in bed.

THE LEO MALE

This guy thinks he looks good, and usually does. Is he charming, of course he is, look at that smile. This is also the ruler of the bedroom, perhaps the whole house.

He may be a braggart of sexual prowess, but he may have a hard time living up to his own high standards. This is a show and tell man, and he loves hearing others tell him how good he is, and how good he looks, even if it is not currently true.

In his later years, if all is not well with his own physical ability, he can deviate into other avenues of interest. He may attempt to continue making love to a woman, or women, to prove to them that he is capable. However, it may be a front for his own needs, that of proving to himself that he can still perform.

This is the actor, the man who can talk his way into bed with the one he has chosen. Once he has this person under his spell, he will work at it to keep them as a personal possession, much like that of a Taurus.

If it takes a continuous stream of gifts, so be it. This is a family man, and one who loves deeply. His chosen mate will, as a rule, be an ordinary woman. After all, he is, and wants to be, the only star to shine in his home.

His love life is pretty much along the lines of straight sex. He does not want to experiment with odd sexual practices. These odd sexual practices are to most other lovers, pretty much accepted and enjoyed, but not to the Leo male. He may in fact, set up dates to make love with his mate.

THE LEO FEMALE

This may be the sexiest looking woman of the Zodiac. She will have an aura about her that draws men to her like bees to honey. No matter her age, she will appear as youthful, and forever able to attract the admiring gaze of a possible suitor. She can tell a bold face lie to a man and he will probably believe every word of it completely.

If you are the male of the species, and trying to attract this woman, good luck. This woman is costly, and not necessarily in a monetary realm. This woman owns her men, perhaps for the rest of their lives, at least in some manner.

They can have moved on from her immediate lifestyle, they may have a new love in their life, they may not even be in the same country, but they still belong to her in some way. And they both know this to be true. As a young woman, she will not be available as a bed partner in her youth, this is someone who determines that life has things to offer her, and she will go after them while she can.

With the natural beauty this woman possesses, is it any wonder why most of the worlds better known female models are of the sun sign Leo. Even as a model showing the entire world what she looks like in the nude, and nudity comes natural to this woman, make no bones about it, this is a sophisticated woman.

Should you be one of the man she has chosen, expect to have a good time when you are with her, in bed, or out on the town. She has a good sense of humor, and is fun to be with. Do not worry about her having a sense of self worth, she may have more self-confidence than the men she encounters.

THE VIRGO MALE

Though a figure of respectability, he can, on occasion, be pulled off the shelf of virtue by the right woman and the right conditions surrounding their relationship. This male will maintain a youthful appearance for most of his life. He is attracted to younger women, and they too him. His intellectual state of mind often comes across as being interested in them mentally, as well as sexually.

A problem can occur in his relationships as the female may think of him as a great potential, and long range lover. I'm told this is true, but this can be a falsehood to the sensuous female, as this is also the natural virgin no matter his age. Though he can, and will enjoy the sexual love life, his better mate will be one with her own intellectual pursuits in life.

To be a lover of a Virgo male, is to be filed away in his mind. A location, where he can, at will, bring forth the mental image of the woman of his choosing. This will include every physical feature no matter how small, or forgotten by others. The feel of her skin, the look of her lips, the shape of her breasts, her sensuous hips, the beauty between her legs, and the abilities of they two of them together as a couple. Because of this ability, this male also fantasizes, and this brings a need of masturbation for satisfaction.

This is a man who generally chooses the correct mate for his life. She may be just what he wants in a mate, but he may not work out to be her best choice. When he does reach old age, he may think, "Where the hell did my life go. I'm not ready to be this age, no matter what age that might be."

THE VIRGO FEMALE

You never know with this woman, is she going to talk your ear off, or have an attitude problem. Either way, it will be done in a tactful manner. You might not even understand some of the words she uses, well at least not the ones she uses in a normal conversation.

This is a learned individual, and you will know this from the way she speaks. She is, what is referred to as, 'Well spoken.' This is a woman who enjoys learning, and does so ceaselessly. She is very much a liberated woman, she needs no one, and that is not a problem for her.

To entice this woman into bed, will take some doing. Do not misunderstand this woman, if she is asking you questions about your sexual abilities, it's not because she wants to go to bed with you, it's because she just wants to know. While you age, she will remain young. Other men may inquire as to how you happen to have such a young lover. She may even be older than you when they ask.

Unlike some sun signs, this woman is not a pushover. If you do become a lover of this woman, you best behave yourself. If not, you will really understand the meaning of 'A woman scorned.' This can be a vengeful person, and it can come from any source, jealousy, or gossip. Even circulating rumors could be your undoing, and true or not.

One of the worst men for this woman, is the Virgo male. The correct man will be one with an aura of charm and magnetism, a special kind of sex appeal, which will induce this female to join him. Quite possibly turning her into a real woman, a woman who will enjoy a love she never thought possible.

She often chooses a man she can dominate, as she wants a man she can teach anything to, but mostly about how to behave in the bedroom. This can be the woman that is similar to the black widow spider, once she's had you, you may be dead meat. She too, like the male Virgo, also fantasizes, and this brings a need of masturbation for self-satisfaction. However, this will not happen as often as it does for other women. She will tell you she really enjoys love making. What she will not be aware of is that her required frequency is often far short of what is considered normal for most others.

Part of her problems stem from the fact that she is a self-perfectionist and if she is perfect, why aren't you. If you have to work around her, it's best to work with her, because you won't last working for her.

THE LIBRA MALE

This man will know about sex in its every form. To this male, sex may be the study hall of nature. This is a man who studies beauty to the point that it is so stimulating to him, that it is almost edible, perhaps even boys, or girls will be on his list. The woman who marries this male, will enjoy him to the fullest.

This, is a man who has a natural magnetism about him that will draw others to him. It may be his looks, his personality, or his physique. No matter the age, this ability will carry through his entire life. Others cannot seem to do enough for him, whether they are asked too, or not.

How many lovers can he have at any one time, as many as he wants. Even though, he will have a problem making decisions in his daily life, there will not be any problems with his love life. He can balance the relationship with every one of his lovers simultaneously. Each of them may offer him some different style of love making, as variety can be his spice of life.

As a youth in school, this male will be sought after by his classmates, young women, older women, and perhaps an interested male. As a rule, this man may marry later in life, but this may be and after he has tried every female he's had a yen for. Women love this man, every woman, and it takes a very good woman to keep him as her own.

THE LIBRA FEMALE

This is a woman who can have what she wants, and quite often when she wants it, and where. This woman will have the qualities of a southern Belle even if raised in a tough neighborhood in any large city, and far from the south. She has a natural charm and grace about her that is uncommon in most women. It is this natural ability to exude charm that brings her what she desires, and without asking. People just can't help themselves, they just want to do things for her.

As an accomplished artist in many fields, this is a woman who tends to place her mate on a pedestal. Oh she will allow him to fall off, but odds are she will put him right back up there, regardless of his faults. Her mate will be the one that makes the world turn.

You won't find this woman in any woman's liberation movement, for she is a woman, and probably the most feminine of our species. To watch her move, is to enjoy the sensuousness of womanhood. Though, to get her into bed, will require real love, as it comes first. You will also have to look like a real man. For this woman, her ideal mate could indeed be another of her own sign, Libra. She understands the sexual appetite, and nothing is above, or below her. Finding no fault with any sexual practice, she can be quite gifted as a lover.

If you wrong this woman, as a lover, don't look for her to remain in your company long, because she is strong and can make it on her own. She is tolerant, and she is patient, that is why she often marries correctly.

THE SCORPIO MALE

There are those who say that the only thing this man thinks about, is sex. Some seem to think he is a walking sex machine, and they are wrong. This may be the case sometimes, but this is not always a true certainty. In fact, there may be times this male will go months without making love.

There is also a distinct possibility that this male of the species, will learn about sex at an early age. The attention he receives will come from both female, and male lovers. At the same time, this can be a very powerful lover in any sexual experience. Rarely a follower, but more often the leader in love making, no matter whom it might be with.

When he tires of a romantic lover in his life, he can abandon a relationship with that person with little hesitation. To do so will not carry any mentally ill feelings, or those of a personal loss in his mind. This male, if born around two O'clock in the afternoon, will have a Pisces rising sign.

When this is the case, this produces a double water sign configuration, and can be trouble. The Scorpio with Pisces rising may seek escape from his troubles by drinking, or by the use of a habitual, or hallucinatory drug.

If you have ever been stung, by the Scorpio Sun sign, you will remember this ex-lover, but these will not be pleasant memories. This ex-lover will be one of those commonly known as, "Old what's his name.' Or, is this something said by those who lack experience with better lovers, because some say this is the best of lovers. The question remains.

THE SCORPIO FEMALE

This woman seems a mystery to many, and because of the mystery, she may be sought out as a lover. In reality she is a mystery because she won't tell anyone anything about herself. Her life is hers alone, and it will not be open for anyone's viewing.

Most water signs let others see them as suffering individuals in some manner. Scorpio is like that too, except the Scorpio will suffer in subtle ways. Oh, make no mistake about it, if the Scorpio woman is suffering in some manner, her lover will suffer in some manner as well. Though they will be different methods of suffering, his may be the worse of the two. At least he will think this is the case.

Consider this scenario, You're married to the Scorpio, and you have an affair outside of the marriage, and she finds out about it. With most other sun signs, the marital partner who strayed from his marital bed is faced with a divorce, and put out of his home. In this first situation, the marriage or relationship is over with.

However, if this happens to a man with a Scorpio wife, there will not be any divorce, at least not from her side of the marriage. Oh no, she'll stay in the marriage to punish the unfaithful mate. The punishment might only be her presence in the marriage, and it will be a punishment. Sex with her after the infidelity can be forgotten.

Most men expect to be the dominant lover in their relationships with women, but not with this woman. If you are involved with this woman, you will be in good shape just to attain a status of 'Equal.' If you really want to experience life, you should experience this woman, well once anyway, and if possible, try to come away un-scathed.

THE SAGITTARIUS MALE

This man can often become known a man's man. A man other men enjoy being around, a sportsman, a storyteller, and a gambler. He can love men, or women, even women of questionable ages. As a gambler, he can spend more money than he can readily afford to spend. But then who knows, 'The long shot might actually win.'

Though this sun sign rules higher education, he may not obtain a great deal of it himself. He will seem well educated, and he will be, but it will not be from schooling in the normal sense of the word. It will be garnered from the others he comes into contact with.

If you are involved with this male, and a major problem arises, do not look for him to bail you out. You better find your own solution to the problem because this male may not have a clue as to what to do, or who to contact for the answers.

Sagittarian men may not find happiness until after their 56th birthday. It seems as if they wait this long to actually begin a settled life style. They are just too busy in the years previous to this part of life to stop having fun. Even if they are having the fun by themselves.

THE SAGITTARIUS FEMALE

This woman has men hovering around her like moths to a flame. They seem to think they need to protect her. Don't you believe it, this is one strong woman. She is self confident, and can attain great heights in the professional world if she so desires. Though she does not search out lovers, she has a continual flame burning that needs only to be fanned to turn it into a roaring blaze. She may not pursue men, but she loves sex when it appears in the correct manner.

Though this woman can be the self made person, she needs a strong male to make her happy in marriage. Not a mate to dominate her, because it cannot be done, but one upon whom she can rely to take care of matters, and to take care of her. He needs to be physically, and mentally strong. Perhaps more on the mental side than the physical.

This is not a woman to make angry, she will quickly put you in your place, and it matters not where you are at the time. The male who can stand up to her, can come out victorious.

THE CAPRICORN MALE

This is, at times, a very difficult man to figure out. Often seen by others as a cold and calculating man, he is in reality a very warm hearted, and romantic person. You may think he all business at parties and meetings, however, while he is there, he is really thinking about the woman he wants to get into his bed. And once he has her, she may keep him.

It is said that this male can become homosexual, but once he discovers how girls are different, other love lifestyle interests are forgotten. For a tender lover, and a lover that is fulfilling, the Capricorn can be a love machine. This may be the only boy who learns, at a very young age, what making love is all about.

Often finding the best marriages after he has turned thirty, but as a lover the older he gets the better he gets. He may seem a social snob, but he can enjoy taking a woman to a hide-a-way motel for a sexual experience she will remember. It is not un-usual for him to carry on an alliance for years, whether or not he is married or single.

With the right mate, he is the kindest, sweetest, and best cheat the world has ever known.

THE CAPRICORN FEMALE

This is a woman who can spend her nights with men, or women. Not only is she a qualified lover for each, but she enjoys it as well. This is not a weak woman by any means. This is a leader of people, men and women alike.

One minute she can give off a 'Come and take me,' look, and the next minute she can seem to be a block of ice. This is an attractive, aristocratic woman. When things start to go to pieces, this woman will react with calm, and control.

If you are the lover of this woman, don't make the mistake of doing wrong by her. If you do, you will openly experience more misery than you ever though possible, well a Virgo Sun sign may be worse.

If you are someone causing problems for this woman's lover, you don't want her to get between the two of you. This is a disaster area just waiting for you to enter.

This is a woman who can carry on secret love affairs for years. It may be the fact, that it is a secret that makes her so hot to have the lover she is involved with.

THE AQUARIUS MALE

Of all of the men who say, "I'm different." this one is truly different. This man does not think in the here and now. This man thinks years ahead, perhaps centuries ahead of others.

He will be an experimenter in sex, he wants to know all about the bedroom pleasures, and he wants to know all about your pleasures as well. He may seem to be a weakling in the eyes of some, but never as a stud. This is an error in thinking, as this man can take care of a harem. Especially if he has Venus in the first house.

His seemingly easy going attitude has led many a mistress into his bed before they even realized they wanted to be there. His body hides more potency, virility, and testosterone than nearly any other sun sign. This is the Casanova of the world. His sexual prowess gives pleasures, which are returned by his wife, mistress, or strangers in the night.

Though this man is widely admired, and deservedly so, as he ages his mind can still make promises his body might have trouble fulfilling. As a younger man, he bestows kindness on the young girls, and the older women, as he ages these are still his best used tools. His attentiveness, and the gallantry, are his best methods in the pursuit of his sexual fantasy, and for the next one he wants to bed.

He will not choose a woman who is not his equal, for this reason he is choosy about any woman he becomes involved with. This, is a man who lives for the moment, now, today. He can make himself at home anywhere in the world, and quickly. This, is a man who makes his own laws, and keeps them.

Some think of him as a simple person, they're wrong again. He can be very complex, yet he can explain his ways to others in a simple manner.

How does he feel about someone, just watch the way he acts around him, or her. He may not be using words, but his actions will speak volumes.

THE AQUARIAN FEMALE

This can be a woman full of surprises, because this woman was born liberated. This woman can hold the whole world in the palm of her hand. Her love of mankind may be so great, that her own family may suffer from lack of her attention.

Men often misunderstand this woman. When they first meet her, they may think she is after their bodies, whereas, in reality this woman only wants to be a friend. This woman may want her sex life to be like the days of old. The Victorian days when there was romance with poetry being read to her by the man of her choice.

When she says, 'Let's get together,' she means to help someone else, not, 'let's go to bed.' But, as a lover of this woman, when you do get to go to bed with her, make sure she gets to snuggle up next to you. This part of the physical touch means a great deal to her, and as her lover the man needs to whisper sweet things in her ear, perhaps even lustful things.

This sun sign is similar to that of Leo in the sense that this can be one of the most beautiful women around. Sometimes their beauty is outward, sometimes it is not to be seen physically, but it is there to be experienced. If her Venus is in the same sign as her chosen mate, he will have an ideal marital partner.

This is the leader of women the world over. What she decides is best for women, is often the correct direction to go for the rest of womankind.

THE PISCES MALE

The Pisces man is loaded with sex appeal no matter what he looks like, or the shape he is in. When the correct woman steps into his close aura field, she may see the bedroom is waiting just for her.

Though he is one of the most introverted of men, he is chivalrous, poetic, and romantic. He has sex pulsing through his entire body. He cares not if the woman is a stunning beauty, he will be lighting her cigarette, getting her another drink, listening to her life story, and enjoying every bit of the connection being made between them.

One of his major problems is anything of a narcotic stimulant. It might be alcohol, or something that has the ability to alter his frustrations. This of course messes up his sexual abilities as well. From this point on, he can go into a downward spiral.

This is a man who can suffer from nearly anything whether he has it or not, the symptoms will appear. He will not go see a doctor, because he might be faced with the fact that he is fine, other than his overuse of mind-altering drugs.

THE PISCES FEMALE

You may never know this woman, not in reality anyway. She is a master of disguise without even trying hard. A Pisces woman, with her unusual light blue eyes, can suck a man right into their very depths. He will be lost from the beginning, as her deceptions will color his world. When he is able to hold her close, he will think it is an illusion, it can't be true that he really has her.

This woman is aware of, and understands the unknown world, as she is herself a part of the illusion. She will show off her natural beauty, and she knows it will attract the male species to her readily. She may search for the perfect man, though it can cost her more than one marriage. She may not even realize she is searching for her father figure.

If she is unhappy, she can disappear in the wink of an eye, and she may not be found. At least not until she is ready to be found. She is so illusionary that a man in her life won't know from one minute to the next, if she is having a attitude problem, or if she just being herself.

Like the Pisces male, her moods can lead to escaping from the real world into one of make believe. If you decide to go drinking with her, she will match you drink for drink, and she'll be the sober one driving you home.

What she really needs is a mate who will give her unrequited love, needing her presence in his life, and possessing her to the point of controlling her, to her satisfaction.

FINDING YOUR MATE

The following listings are basic factors only, but I think you will find them of interest. If used correctly, you should be able to decide which might be the better mate to have in your life.

We will start out with the fundamentals of Sun sign compatibility's, and then we will expand further into other influences. The beliefs are that the air signs do well with the fire signs, and that the earth signs are better off with the water signs. Then we'll discuss the same elements being together, that is fire to fire, earth to earth, air to air, and water to water.

When you have found your own Sun sign, and the list of which Sun signs are suggested for your consideration, you also need to determine which ascending sign is best for you. The ascending sign is determined by the time of day the person is born.

The ascending sign is important because it determines what kind of personality the individual possesses. The Sun sign is a person's individuality.

Sun Signs	Signs and their compatibility by their elements		
Fire sign Aries	March 21 to April 20		
	Gemini	Libra	Aquarius
Earth sign Taurus	April 21 to May 21		
	Cancer	Scorpio	Pisces
Air sign Gemini	May 22 to June 22		
	Aries	Leo	Sagittarius
Water sign Cancer	June 23 to July 22		
	Taurus	Virgo	Capricorn
Fire sign Leo	July 23 to August 22		
	Gemini	Libra	Aquarius
Earth sign Virgo	August 23 to September 22		
	Cancer	Scorpio	Pisces
Air sign Libra	September 23 to October 22		
	Aries	Leo	Aquarius
Water sign Scorpio	October 23 to November 21		
	Taurus	Virgo	Capricorn

Fire sign	November 22 to December 21		
Sagittarius	Gemini	Libra	Aquarius
Earth sign	December 22 to January 19		
Capricorn	Cancer	Scorpio	Pisces
Air sign	January 20 to February 18		
Aquarius	Aries	Leo	Sagittarius
Water sign	February 19 to March 20		
Pisces	Taurus	Virgo	Capricorn

FIRE & FIRE

Fire signs involved with fire signs can create way too much heat. Both signs will want to be the leader, and neither will be willing to give in to the others demands. This is just trouble waiting to happen. However, if you decide to mix fire with fire, or fight fire with fire as the case may be, look for the following birth times for one of the following people. Doing this will provide the fire sign with an air ascending sign. At least doing this gives the relationship a chance of survival.

The hours listed are the odd hours. Using this method should find the better ascending sign for the partner in each case. However, the closer to the even hour in the middle, the better the chance for the air sign ascendant. As an example,

Aries born between the hours of 9:00 AM to 11:00 AM will, as a rule, have Gemini on the ascendant if there is not an intercepted sign involved. The middle hour would be 10:00 AM. An even numbered hour.

Aries 9:00 AM - 11:00 AM will have a Gemini ascendant.

Aries 5:00 PM - 7:00 PM will have a Libra ascendant.

Aries 1:00 AM - 3:00 AM will have an Aquarius ascendant.

Leo 1:00 AM - 3:00 AM will have a Gemini ascendant.

Leo 9:00 AM - 11:00 AM will have a Libra ascendant.

Leo 5:00 PM - 7:00 PM will have an Aquarius ascendant.

Sagittarius 5:00 PM - 7:00 PM will have an Gemini ascendant.

Sagittarius 1:00 AM - 3:00 AM will have an Libra ascendant

Sagittarius 9:00 AM - 11:00 AM will have an Aquarius ascendant

ARIES
The air signs of Gemini, Libra, and Aquarius, will fan the flames of an Aries.

The water signs of Cancer, Scorpio, and Pisces will find them too hot to handle, I'm sure you've heard of being in hot water.

The earth signs of Virgo and Capricorn will feel like baked clay. For them, an Aries holds no interest.

LEO
The other fire signs of Aries and Sagittarius can work well for a Leo, if the ascending sign is considered, and well placed.

You would think the air signs of Gemini, Libra, and Aquarius would blow out the flames of a Leo, but they might just fan them into a higher flame.

Pisces can not match Leo's needs, and Taurus, Virgo, and Capricorn are too down to earth for a Leo.

As mentioned before, Leo and Cancer can make good mates, but as the saying goes, test the waters.

SAGITTARIUS

Pisces could work out as mate for this sign, if the ascending sign is compatible. Unfortunately, this sun sign often suffers from multiple marriages because they take too much time analyzing the potential mate. Instead, they should just let things work themselves out.

The sign of Sagittarius, and that of Aquarius, need personal freedoms. The more a potential mate, or marriage partner tries to fence these signs in, the more they rebel. Give them freedom, and they can become steadfast.

The other fire signs, Aries, and Leo can be good mates, but the ascending sign should be considered to help with the harmony.

Air signs, Gemini, Libra, and Aquarius are compatible, because they have wide interests, and share the intellectual side of Sagittarius.

The other water signs of Cancer, and Scorpio will not understand the Sagittarian's needs for freedom or solitude. These water signs are emotional signs, and as they themselves may enjoy some solitude, to find others who need time alone will surprise them. Most often the water signs are too emotional for the Sagittarian.

The earth signs of Taurus, Virgo and Capricorn might do well as business partners, but they should be avoided as lifetime mates.

EARTH & EARTH

Earth signs are better off with water signs, but they can mix well together. Taurus earth may be from a farm, Virgo earth is probably potting soil, and Capricorn earth comes from a good neighborhood, but dirt is dirt.

Taurus born between the hours of 5:00 PM to 7:00 PM will, as a rule, find Scorpio on the ascendant. The middle even hour would be 6:00 PM.

Taurus 9:00 AM - 11:00 AM will have a Cancer ascendant.

Taurus 5:00 PM - 7:00 PM will have a Scorpio ascendant.

Taurus 1:00 AM - 3:00 AM will have a Pisces ascendant.

Virgo 1:00 AM - 3:00 AM will have a Cancer ascendant.

Virgo 9:00 AM - 11:00 AM will have a Scorpio ascendant.

Virgo 5:00 PM - 7:00 PM will have a Pisces ascendant.

Capricorn 5:00 PM - 7:00 PM will have an Cancer ascendant.

Capricorn 1:00 AM to 3:00 AM will have an Scorpio ascendant.

Capricorn 9:00 AM - 11:00 AM will have an Pisces ascendant.

TAURUS

Virgo and Capricorn may bring successes into the marriage, as long as they do not look for emotional wonderment.

It is possible that over time, the water signs can suck the life out of a Taurus mate.

The signs of Gemini and Libra, often bewilder a Taurus, as they are just too scattered to suit the steadfast nature of this earth sign.

VIRGO

This might be a questionable mix, because fire and earth are not natural elements, but Leo can be a very good mate for this sign, as the Virgo understands the Leo's need to shine.

Though the other earth signs of Taurus, and Capricorn can be good mates for Virgo, they are not as strong, Cancer, Scorpio and Pisces may provide a better sex life for the Virgo than any other sign.

The signs of Aries, and Sagittarius are just to hot for a Virgoan to handle. This could be like the game of 'Hot potato, hot potato.'

CAPRICORN

Cancer could be one of the best mates for a Capricorn. This is the teacher, and among other things, sex is one of their favorite things to teach. However, with Venus in Capricorn, this can be a sign of sexual greed.

Taurus, and Virgo could become good mates for this sign as well.

The water signs, Scorpio, and Pisces are also good potential mates for a Capricorn.

The air signs, Gemini, Libra, and Aquarius may not do well with this sign, because Capricorn may be too down to earth for their likes.

The fire signs can communicate well with this sign, but, odds are marital bliss will not be forthcoming.

AIR & AIR

Air signs do well together, at least platonically. There is some question as to whether or not they can be depended on staying true to one another. They may seek the fire signs to warm them.

Gemini 9:00 AM - 11:00 AM will have a Leo ascendant.

Gemini 1:00 AM - 3:00 AM will have an Aries ascendant.

Gemini 5:00 PM - 7:00 PM will have a Sagittarius ascendant.

Libra 1:00 AM - 3:00 AM will have a Leo ascendant.

Libra 5:00 PM - 7:00 PM will have an Aries ascendant.

Libra 9:00 PM - 11:00 PM will have a Sagittarius ascendant.

Aquarius 5:00 PM - 7:00 AM will have an Leo ascendant.

Aquarius 9:00 AM - 11:00 AM will have an Aries ascendant.

Aquarius 1:00 AM - 3:00 AM will have an Sagittarius ascendant.

GEMINI

Virgo is often a good mate for this sign, as it is one of mutual intellectual pursuits. Though in many writings this will not be the recommended combination.

The air signs, Libra and Aquarius are also good possibilities for Gemini as mates.

The signs of Scorpio and Pisces are way too emotional for a Gemini, there would be little chance of a permanent union between this combination.

There is little hope for an interest between a Gemini, and a Taurus, or that of a Capricorn. A dust storm brings a good picture to mind with this combination.

LIBRA

If it is to be an air sign combination for Libra, try Aquarius as a first choice, then Gemini.

Aries, Leo, and Sagittarius, can be good with a Libra, as this is a combination where the air sign of Libra can really light the fires of the fire signs.

Libra is not good with the water signs, Cancer, Scorpio, or Pisces. They are too emotional to satisfy this air sign.

Capricorn's and Libra's rarely work out as a good combination.

AQUARIUS

Libra may be their best marital mate. This is the last sign to ever suffer from social immoralities of any kind. They are rarely frustrated, and usually find great pleasure in sexual relationships.

They will not do well with the water signs Cancer, Scorpio, and Pisces. The water signs just cannot comprehend the sign of Aquarius. And Aquarians may seem too aloof for a water sign.

The earth signs of Taurus, Virgo, and Capricorn might do well in business with this sign, but not in marriage unless they have similar Venus positions.

The fire signs, Aries, Leo, and Sagittarius can make good mates for Aquarius, as the air sign of Aquarius can fuel the fires of these signs.

WATER & WATER

These signs are too emotional to get along together. Each of them will feel the need to express their emotions, but often they find the other water sign has beat them to center stage.

Cancer 9:00 AM - 11:00 AM will have a Virgo ascendant.

Cancer 1:00 AM - 3:00 AM will have a Taurus ascendant.

Cancer 5:00 PM - 7:00 PM will have a Capricorn ascendant.

Scorpio 1:00 AM - 3:00 AM will have a Virgo ascendant.

Scorpio 5:00 PM - 7:00 PM will have a Taurus ascendant.

Scorpio 9:00 AM - 11:00 AM will have a Capricorn ascendant.

Pisces 5:00 PM - 7:00 PM will have an Virgo ascendant.

Pisces 9:00 AM - 11:00 AM will have an Taurus ascendant.

Pisces 1:00 AM - 3:00 AM will have an Capricorn ascendant.

CANCER

Capricorn may be one of the best signs for Cancer, though the water might get muddy. The Cancer woman might get along well with a Gemini, but the Cancer male will not.

The water signs of Scorpio, and Pisces, can seem very passionate for a Cancer sun sign, and may cause emotional problems which will need to be worked out to be successful.

When it comes to the fire signs, Aries and Sagittarius will not be impressed with a mate who continues to put out their flames with emotionalism.

Leo, on the other hand, has a chance as a potentially good mate. As Cancer rules the home, and Leo rules the children. This combination may require a compatible ascending sign, perhaps even a complimentary Moon sign.

Libra and Aquarius might find the emotional side of this Sign a restrictive factor.

SCORPIO

Virgo can be the best sign for a Scorpio. This is a learned, and sophisticated sex partner, but a sexual game player. As they grow older, sex kind of takes a back seat with these two. It's as if they found out that sex was not what they thought it was going to be.

Cancer and Pisces can work out as mates for Scorpio as they share many traits, and many emotions.

Taurus and Capricorn can get along as mates with a Scorpio as, like Virgo, they are earth signs, and steadfast. The air signs do not work well with Scorpio, mainly because Scorpio can be to sexually demanding, or to forceful.

The air signs will not put up with the ongoing Scorpio's questions about where they have been, or whom they were with. Even if they were doing nothing out of order.

Aries, Leo, and Sagittarius would be a constant battle, rather than mutual agreements.

PISCES

A Sagittarian maybe their best chance at a good marriage, and a happy life, if the ascending signs are compatible. For a Pisces to be really happy, love is a requirement. They cannot give of themselves without love being involved. Though, most of the sun signs find a Pisces can be hard to handle.

The other waters signs of Cancer, and Scorpio can also get on well with a Pisces.

The earth signs, Taurus, Virgo, and Capricorn can be good for the Pisces, but Pisces may not be that good for them.

The air signs of Gemini, Libra, and Aquarius will just bring a chilled wind to the Pisces.

The fire signs, Aries, and Leo, may just evaporate a Pisces psyche because of their intense heat.

WOMEN SEEKING MEN

When a woman is seeking a man, she will use a method that is unique only unto that individual woman. However, as with the men, personal behavior patterns can be detected.

Astrologically speaking, there are twelve basic types of women; still you should keep in mind that most often women think very much like men think. The women you encounter with the healthiest sexual appetites will have the Planet Venus in the signs of Aries, Scorpio, Capricorn and Aquarius.

To learn this information about someone, you will need to know their personal birth time, date, and the place of birth. With this information you can contact an Astrologer to find out which sign Venus was in at the time of their birth. In many cases you can also find this information on the internet, by simply typing *'Ephemeris'* this is a planetary catalog of planet placements.

This kind of knowledge about men can be beneficial to a woman seeking a compatible mate, but it can be a problem if it is used incorrectly. Many women think they are quite capable of handling any man that comes their way, and this is the wrong approach to life. Some of these men will be way out of the woman's league. The key to using this information is in using it wisely.

THE MEN

ARIES

These are aggressive and assertive men. These individuals will pursue you relentlessly. This man is interested in results, do not expect much foreplay ahead of time. For entertainment, this man will take you to events that may require daring on your part. Such as white water river rafting, Bungee jumping, four wheeling in a jeep with the guys, sky diving, hang gliding and any other similar events.

If you are withdrawn, a fraidy cat, or afraid of getting hurt, stay home. Of course, it is possible that this is what has drawn him toward you, or you to him. If you are a single mother with children, you need to ask yourself, are your children dare devils, or do they prefer the quiet of good music, a book, or local theater.

TAURUS

Honesty is an important factor with this man, and it's possible that most social formalities will seem dull to him. When these men are ready to make love, they want to make love right then; they do not want to discuss it first. As this fellow courts you, It could be dinner at a fast food place, or it could be at a very elegant restaurant. You may not know which it will be until you arrive.

Possessions mean a great deal to this person. He may be a frugal spender, but he will acquire the the things he desires. He will drive a very good automobile; wear expensive clothes and may treat you lavishly. After the courtship is over however, you will probably see a change in his spending habits, as this man does not acquire wealth by spending it.

To a child, this is a parent who really loves them, almost to a fault, because of his tendency to over protect them. Protected to the point, that they may not learn life's lessons on their own, or by personal experience until after they leave home. There may be a tendency for this man to smother his mate, and over protect her as well. This is a very independent person, and very set in his ways.

GEMINI

A smooth talker, and one that may try to sweep you off your feet with their vast knowledge. Granted they are smart, but they normally learn a little bit about everything, but not a great deal about any one subject.

This, is the person who will con you out of things with a glib tongue, even if you are not ready to give them up. These items may range from the physical to the materialistic items. When you become involved with this person, don't just give them whatever it seems they may need. Be sure they really need it first.

What this man may tell you is one thing, the complete truth may be quite another. This is a mental person, and the mind works constantly. New things are of interest, but they will tire of the same thing if it's repeated time and again. The foreplay to making love may be extensive, verbally communicated, even fantasy, and will include sensitive touching.

CANCER

This is a real homebody, and one that will take you to his place to cook dinner for you. Let him, odds are you will enjoy it, but domestic is the key word here. This man is not one for going out to dinner a great deal. The home and the family are utmost in this man's mind.

He makes a commitment to a relationship, and one of dedication to a lasting union. In the event there is a snag in the affair, he will continue to try working things out as long as his partner is similarly dedicated. To be unfaithful to this man is to create a great wrong.

This can be a moody man. You will find out, that when it is warm and sunny outside, he will be in good humor. If it is cloudy, foggy, rainy or similar weather, he can be moody and down. This man will have gone through many different problems in his lifetime and he will understand the problems of others.

LEO

Here is the true family man, one who believes in having children, and spending quality time with them. This is also very out going man. He will buy you gifts in his attempts to win your affections. You may not feel indebted to him, but that will be one of his methods of winning you.

This, is the man who wants quality things for show and tell. You may become one of those prized items. He will treat you well, and give you material possessions, but you may be one of his. This is one of the more handsome looking signs of the zodiac, and he is an independent individual.

You need to know the inner being, as this Sun sign can hide their true nature. Their love nature can seem playful.

VIRGO

This man may actually pursue you for your intellect. He, himself, will be an intellectual and a learned person. He can also be very much the critic, the one who will criticize your faults trying to make you better. But praise will also come forth for your better qualities. This, is the person who is overly neat and meticulous in every way, and the perfect gentleman.

There will be trips to the museums, libraries, or other places of knowledge. He may also have some tendency toward health conditions. Or he could be someone who suffers from hypochondria.

There could be some unusual conditions in this man's love life. Marriage itself, may not be an important factor in his life.

When he finds out what it is you like in a lover, he will try to become the best lover you have ever experienced. If you want variety, you will need to convey this message to this man as a lover. For him fantasy will cause excitement. Such as an invitation to take a shower with you. His imagination can cover many sexual situations for you to enjoy, he will enjoy them as well. There are those who think of these men as cold in bed, and there are those who think this is one of the best of lovers.

LIBRA

This person is interested in the arts. And an art form, of some kind, will be evident in his life style. He may also dress in the latest fashion, or he could just as easily be very sloppy. The problem you will encounter here is that you will have to make the decisions as to which stage play you would like to see, or chose which of the fine restaurants at which you would like to dine. This fellow will have trouble making up his mind about many things, which shirt to wear, which tie, where to go for dinner, should he get gas for the car now, or wait until after he picks you up.

When he does make up his mind, it can seem as if it will be with difficulty, and so the choices may be left up to you. He is a quiet person, but he does enjoy social affairs. To entice this man, try perfume and satin sheets. Don't be surprised by the inventiveness of love situations you may encounter. Before you allow yourself to get deeply involved with this man, understand what it is he expects from you as a lover. Sometimes his idea of the perfect lover is a bit lofty.

SCORPIO

This man will want to know all about you. The questions, as he asks them, may be subtle, but continuous, and yet he will give you very little information about himself. He feels as though, that if he gives away personal information, he will give the other person too great a hold, or advantage over him.

He will take you to a cozy little hideaway for the weekend, or to isolated beaches. Quiet out of the way places, as this person enjoys the quiet solitude. This can be an intense lover, perhaps even unconventional. Jealousy could be in abundance with this man as well. Mood swings may take place, and you will never know why. But you will be left with the feeling it is your fault, whether it is your fault or not.

SAGITTARIUS

Here is the sports fan. A very outgoing man, but when you are traveling in his company, it will be football games, basketball, sailing, ski trips, or any of the many sporting events. Gambling could be an issue with this person, and he can be a very theological minded man as well. He enjoys the home life and entertaining in the home. Even then, when the games are on, he will be in the den watching them on television, perhaps his male friends will be there also.

Promiscuity takes place in many forms, and this man may exercise some of them. If you experience anger coming from this person during any part of your relationship, analyze your relationship carefully before any long-term commitments are made.

As a lover he will take what comes naturally at the time, whatever that may be.

CAPRICORN

This is a social man, and someone who can be deeply involved in the business community. This man may well have his own business or be in a favored position in a business that requires a social indulgence. He has a great sense of humor, and an easy manner about him. This is a down to earth person, one who thinks logically, and can at times seem somewhat boring depending on the company around him at the time.

He prefers long term relationships in is life, the term "One night stands," usually will not apply here. Don't be afraid of being the leader in this romance, it is acceptable. If this relationship starts to deteriorate, do not expect to hold it together with sex, sex alone will not work.

AQUARIUS

This is a man who you will rarely find to be dull, and you will never know what is about to take place next in life with this man. This one thinks well into the future, and way ahead of most others. This is possibly one of the most attractive looking men of the zodiac.

This man may take you to a fast food place for lunch and a then a very nice place for dinner. You may be in for a movie for the evenings entertainment, or perhaps live theater, a museum, or even a planetarium for something different. This unusual individual can cry during a thirty second television commercial, and seem cold toward others the next. This is a shy individual, and he can enjoy solitude as well. Very independent, self sufficient, and rebels against the norm. Therefore, when it comes to this person as a lover, you can experiment and use your imagination. To do so will produce some very enjoyable and memorable love experiences.

Be aware of yourself with this man, he will show you things about yourself you were never aware of before, if you'll let him. This man will find pleasure in giving you pleasure. You will gain more self-gratification by learning to pleasure him as well, and don't be bashful. He will enjoy it if you make the play first.

PISCES

There may be some unusual times with this individual, and he can be moody. You might be able to see his moods change in the depth of his eyes. And at times he will seem to know what is about to happen before it takes place. This man can easily go unnoticed by others entirely. He will enjoy the water, and living around, or on it, as it has a soothing affect on him.

He can be a very social, or a secluded person. This is often the one man who other people talk too about their own problems. His physical involvement's are in tune with his emotional involvement's. He may be drawn into any kind of love situation just to get closer to his mate. This man needs to be aware of his mate, and her intentions, as he can lose himself in the relationship.

MEN SEEKING WOMEN

When a man is seeking a woman he will use a method that is unique only unto that individual man. However, behavior patterns can be detected. Astrologically speaking, there are twelve basic types of men. Still, you should keep in mind that men think very much like women think.

The women with the healthiest sexual appetites, will most often have the Planet Venus in the signs of Aries, Scorpio, Capricorn or Aquarius. To learn this information about someone you will need to know their personal birth time, the date, and their place of birth. With this information, you can contact an Astrologer to find out which sign Venus was in at the time of their birth. In many cases you can also find this information on the internet, by simply typing *'Ephemeris'* this is a planetary catalog of planet placements.

This knowledge about women can be beneficial to a man seeking a compatible mate, but it can be a problem if it is used incorrectly. Many men think they are quite capable of handling any woman that comes into their life, and this is the wrong approach to life's realities. Some of these women will be way out of a man's league, and if the choice is wrong, he will suffer. The key to using this information is in using it wisely.

THE WOMEN

ARIES

These are women who possess strong personalities, to think of this as a namby pamby woman is an error. This is not a woman just any man can get along with. This woman is not going to try to be your equal, she is your equal. She is smart, and can work you into the ground, and then she will wonder why you cannot keep up with her. After all, she is only a woman.

You will probably be drawn to her personal magnetism and charisma, but you must remember, she will not be stopping to take care of you, she has things to get done in her life. If this woman wants you, odds are she'll have you. Then, if you don't measure up, she'll discard you just as quickly. If she starts an argument with you, it will be to see if you are strong enough to stand up to her, if you cave in mercilessly, you loose.

This woman may ask you point blank if you want to go to bed with her, and odds are this is not a test. Either you do, or you don't. It often surprises men how she can be so blunt in her approach, but that is the way she behaves when she feels the need. She may invite a man who interests her, to do something daring. If he hesitates, she may feel that she should not waste anymore time on her pursuit on this male.

TAURUS

A Taurus woman needs a man who is stable, intelligent, and energetic. He needs to be sensitive, and have a good imagination. He will need good common sense, and be able to provide for her well being. The man who patronizes this woman will not get very far with her, she is much to strong for that. The man of her choice will never forget a birthday, an anniversary of any kind. He will cuddle her, comfort her, and compliment her when it is deserved. Will she be a jealous woman? most likely.

This is a quiet woman, one who is composed, who seems as if time has no end. However, when she gets into the bedroom she becomes another woman. When this woman decides you are her next conquest, don't expect it to be a quick session. To satisfy her needs may take a section of your day. Like all morning, or perhaps all afternoon, or all night. A Taurus woman is an artist in several ways. It can be painting, pottery, sculpting, or whatever, but in bed she is indeed an artist. She likes bedding a man because it feels good and it is a natural thing to do.

She will seduce men through many avenues. It could be the low cut dresses she wears, which allows men to gaze down upon her cleavage, perhaps even her breasts. Men never tire of watching her hips as she walks, and she is good at this kind of seduction. Or, is it the way she crosses her legs, or the bedroom eyes. To respond to this woman, pat her on the butt, kiss her on the neck, and touch her somewhere, anywhere, but somewhere.

Perhaps whisper how you would enjoy making love to her in the park after dark, but mean it when you say it, because she will expect it to take place.

GEMINI

This woman can make friends anywhere and anytime, but she will not make a special issue of finding men, and the ones who approach her will be scrutinized carefully. She is suspicious of those who seem to cater to her, but she can entertain men, and several at a time. It's not the quality of men that interests her, it's the quantity of them.

You may seem to be a chosen one, one day, and then you are out of the running the next. Prostitution could be a tried adventure, but probably not lasting long.

A Gemini woman wants a man who can talk to her for hours, and about anything. Then perhaps, a good time can be had in bed, but soon afterward, she will forget all about it until some other time.

This is not a woman, who is not going to dwell on the subject of love making. She is a woman many people have trouble keeping up with, as she is always thinking of her next direction in life. She may go on a trip, and upon her return she'll start right where she left off, as if it was just the day before.

This woman is gifted with the spoken word, and she can join a conversation of any kind, at any time. However, when the conversation starts getting into depth of a particular subject, she is likely to move along to another group discussing yet another topic. It is not that she has gotten bored with the first group, it is because they may have outdistanced her knowledge on the subject at hand. This, is not a woman to confide in with your specific personal problems, as she can be a gossip.

If this is the case, your life's issues may get passed along to someone else as a topic of discussions. However, the story, as told to her, will have changed so much, that even you may have trouble recognizing them as being yours.

CANCER

As a man, you will find this woman wants you to proceed at a slow pace with her, as she cannot be rushed. She will insist that she is the only one in your life, and without this condition in place, a man will not keep her. She may seem to be a weak woman, but this is not the case. She will seek a man who can take complete care of her, emotionally, and financially.

When she has the right male in her life, her sexual appetite will be open to nearly any avenue, as long as it is just the two of you. Once you have an established relationship with a Cancer Sun sign woman, you can make love to this woman from the front, back, top or bottom, and she is open to oral, or anal sex. She may be the wettest woman between the legs you've ever made love to, and she likes making love anywhere it might be wet. Such as showers, outside in the rain, on the beach, in a pond, you name it. She does like romantic settings so use them, candles, a fire in the fireplace, silk sheets on the bed, champagne and anything else along these lines.

She will not tolerate a rough man; a man who treats women harshly, as this is a sensitive woman. She prefers a man who will take the initiative, but once aroused she can easily take the lead. The man in her life will have to understand her moods, because she will have them, probably forever. It will be an understanding that he cannot ask her what is wrong, because odds are she won't know herself. This woman will commitment to a relationship with lasting dedication, and to be unfaithful to this person is to create a great wrong.

LEO

This woman talks a good story, but she often lacks the ability to perform as good as she lets others believe she can. She likes her sex and her love life to be intertwined together, but in her life, this may not always be the case. Usually she is a devoted wife, until, or unless things in her life are falling apart.

There is no question this is an attractive woman, and she knows she has an impact on men. She will look for a man who treats her like a queen, one who heaps praise upon her, and buys her jewelry. If you wish to pursue this woman, you better not be a cheapskate. If you become this woman's lover, and if you are a good lover, this woman can become a wildcat in bed. She likes oral sex, she likes to be on top, and may enjoy pornographic films and stories.

She will treat the man in her life with visual views of her in flimsy night wear, or you may just as easily find her completely nude. This is the natural exhibitionist, and nudity is an enjoyable state to her. This could be a woman who flashes her open legs to a man passing by her car as she opens the door. Will she be wearing underwear, maybe, maybe not. As a man, you must understand that this woman enjoys foreplay, perhaps more than the act of making love itself.

VIRGO

This is a woman who will look for a man whom she can help, or benefit him in any way she can. This is the perfect woman, if you doubt this, just ask her. This is not someone to start a relationship with just any man, as she will take her time to find the perfect lover for herself. Though her passions may take awhile to burst into flames, the potential lover just has to wait for the event to take place. She will insist on being perfect in her lovemaking. She will learn everything about the man of her choice, so she can fill every need he may have. All she needs is to find the time to do these things.

When she falls in love, it will be a deep love, a lasting love. She does have a drawback, which is the fact she seems to be a magnet for the wrong kind of men. Many may be restrictive to her in some manner, though she may subconsciously seek these men out to fulfill her need to take care of them. There are those who think of these women as cold in bed, and there are those who think this is one of the best of lovers.

LIBRA

This is a classy lady, in the bedroom or out. She likes men to be informed, and can hold her own in a good conversation. She often finds herself interested in older men, intelligent men, and men of good taste. This is not a woman that just any man is going to get into bed.

This woman takes more than just some sweet talk, it may take several things, or perhaps very little, but it will take something. Perhaps a dinner for two, an evening at the theater, a good wine by the fireplace, or, maybe just a good conversation. She does not expect to open her own doors, the man in her life is expected to do that for her, and he better be well groomed. Being dressed sloppily and taking her to a bar is not going to work well to entice her. Spoil her with gifts, and she will spoil you.

This is an attractive woman, she may not be a raving beauty, but men will notice her. Though this is not someone who lives for sex, she exudes it in her walking, and mannerisms. She has hips that are provocative as she moves, and she smells good. Once you have her in bed, you can use sexually explicit language, and a mirror over the bed will be welcome.

SCORPIO

This may seem unfair, but whatever this woman does for her mate, she will expect to get something in return. At some point, the man in her life will have to pay for her services one way or another. As a mate to this woman, you will never know her fully, as she keeps personal secrets about herself wholly unto her. She will become her mate's right hand, and she does this to protect her own future.

A weak male will not fare well with this strong woman, as a weak male will not be able to keep up with her demands. If you cannot produce what this woman wants, when she finds out you are not the man she thought you were, she could make your life miserable. However, the myth of the Scorpio woman can be just that, a myth. This is not always a heavily sexed sign, in fact it can be quite the opposite. She does however, control the sexual portion of her life. Sometimes to her own dismay.

SAGITTARIUS

To love this woman, is to love a challenge. To keep her is equally a task. Her independence requires her lovers, or mates, allow her unquestionable freedom. This woman, and the Aquarian, are two Sun signs that are not like other women. They can fall in love, and deeply, but it is not unusual for them to keep sex and love as separate parts of their lives. If you have been a lover of one of these women, you will know how lucky you have been, and to have had her once, is to remember her forever.

If you want to know this woman, very well, you better like the out of doors, and if you want to chat with her, expect to do so at some kind of sporting event. To get to know her around the office can be hard to do, as she is a ball of fire and energy. To tie her down long enough to make a connection is trying, and if your want to know what she thinks of you, all you need do is ask. Be aware however, sometimes the truth can be brutal.

If she wants you, odds are you will know it before the actual conquest takes place. She can be ready to make love in a very short time; in fact, she is ready nearly anytime. Once you are in this woman's life, don't try to fence her in, if you attempt to do this, you will find yourself with an empty corral. To approach this woman, you need to be direct, don't beat around the bush with her, and if you are a weak male, you won't get to the bedroom with her. You have to be strong, but do not confuse strength with that of a cave man, because this is not the kind of strength she looks for in a partner.

CAPRICORN

This is a woman, who, under the right circumstances, can shed a mate without so much as a backward glance. This won't happen often in her life, but it can happen. She can live a solitary lifestyle, but would rather not. The older she gets, the more sexually appealing she can be. As a child, she is often the tomboy that is overlooked as a real girl, and boys do not take her seriously when it comes to her feminine nature. She is also a daddy's girl. Yet, as an adult, she can be more woman than many other females. Don't mistake this woman as 'Just a woman,' this woman is a schemer, a doer, and she will be successful in some manner. It might be as a business CEO or running her own business, but she is thinking professionally when others around her are merely plodding along.

She can be shy, and a very devoted lover when love is found. She can choose the wrong mate in that she may choose losers, but if someone takes unfair advantage of her, it will not be forgotten. This woman is the one who suggests to the man, that she has chosen, that, Perhaps We should get together sometime,' and this is exactly what she means.

When she finds out what the man in her life likes about a woman, be it legs, breasts, hips, long hair, or whatever, she will dress in such a manner as to enhance that part of herself. She is drawn to older men because she feels that they know how to treat a woman, but she will not give of herself easily. What she finds attractive is a man who has old-fashioned values, with a touch of class, and is a gentleman.

AQUARIUS

This woman is not impressed by the strong athletic type of men. She prefers men who are interesting, and cultured. She can join any conversation, and is soon in control of the discussion, or the topic of the discussion. She cares not, if a man has sex appeal, as she knows how to awaken the appetite of the men who know about women.

She may seem, or may be, egotistical and arrogant. Yet she has the smarts to back it up. It doesn't matter as she will be the center of attraction. Whether she has been placed there by others, or by bringing herself into the limelight. You may never know who this woman is from week to week. She might be one of the sixties hippie's type one day, and a well spoken high class woman of quality the next.

Does this woman have morals, absolutely, well at least until they get in her way. If her marriage or relationship is suffering, she may find herself interested in other men, men who are intellectually attractive. You must understand, this woman is a very dedicated partner, but, she doesn't confuse love and sex, because she is well aware they are two completely separate and different things.

If you want to entertain this woman, you better expect to be doing something different. Something unusual, and something outside of the realm of what is considered the norm. As an example, where you might take one woman to a movie, you take the Aquarian woman to a show at the planetarium. Where you go for a drive with other women, you take this woman sailing. I think you get the picture.

PISCES

This woman can be sexually demanding, or unpredictable in her sexual needs. Her sexual needs may differ, and they may come and go. She may find fulfillment often, then she may do without for a length of time. This condition can drive her and her mate to an uneasy relationship. She can easily live in a world of fantasy and may not dare leave it for the reality of life.

The man who has an imagination, and is exploratory, has a good chance in winning this woman. The right man will find himself with a sex slave, or, does he become the sex slave during their lovemaking? At times she can be slow to try new things, but once she finds the pleasure in them, they will become more to her liking. This can really be the whore in the bedroom, and the quiet maiden in the living room.

If you become her first mate, you should know she can discover you are not whom she thought you were, and you can just as easily become history. If you are her second mate, you stand a better chance, but you have to accept her the way she is. Do not offer any rejection, if you do, you may also become history. It's not that she can't take rejection, but to do so it must be done in a constructive manner.

TRANSSEXUALS

When a person decides to make a sex change in their life, it affects a great many people. Almost always, the decision is as hard on the individual as those who are intimate with that individual. Intimate, in the loving as a friend, a relative, or as a lover.

This is not an overnight decision. This kind of thought process can start as young as three years of age. I'm sure this will surprise most everyone, but when thinking about it astrologically, understanding it will be easier. The process goes on continually throughout life, but the basics are as follows:

At the age of three, the Point of Self is passing through the second house of personal wealth. This is not always the house of toys in the child's beginning years, it is also the house of personal self worth, or that of being worthy. Some would argue that a child this young cannot know, or understand, self worth. This line of thinking is ridiculous. Anyone with a lick of sense in the astrological field understands that the first seven years of our lives are the more important in all of life's future decisions.

There is an interim age involved here, and it takes place between the ages of nine years four months and eleven years eight months. These are the years of first loves. When a physical attraction starts it can be jarring for the person to find they are, or want to be, involved with a person of the same sex.

The next critical stage is during the passage of the Point of Self through the sixth house the first time. The sixth house because it involves personal health issues, among many other things, but these are the more dangerous years for young adolescents. These are the years more common with a new knowledge of sex taking place in the young mind. It is not always pleasant at this age. Rape can be a harsh awakening, or that of a sexually transmitted disease, even the mind may be affected.

The third stage, and the more agonizing, is passage by the Point of Self through the fifth house the second time, which is the ages thirty-seven years four months to thirty-nine years and eight months. The fifth house being the house of love, is also the house of gambling. This becomes a key issue, the taking a chance on becoming the real person they want to be.

Once they have made the mental decision, and it almost has to be made now, the passage of Point of Self through the next house, the sixth, may find the sex change taking place. The sixth house this time will encompass the ages of thirty-nine years eight months to forty-two years. With this transit by age the person is going through a house of restriction, and personal health issues. They are by age in opposition to the twelfth house of hospitalization. Mars has to be a factor, as will the Sun and Moon.

The questions remain when passing through the seventh and eighth houses the second time, and the ages of forty-two to forty-six years and eight months are taking place. By age, the Point of Self is passing in opposition to the first house and that of the physical being, and the second house of personal self worth.

This is the time of life when most people encounter a mid-life crisis, and a mid-life crisis taking place for this person can be confusing at best.

The planetary involvement can now be extensive and aspects should be considered, however, unless the individual is in touch with an astrologer, he/she, cannot plan for the better time to make the change. Even if this was the case, the planning can be restricted to the two-year four month window. Why would this window of time be a factor? Because Mother Nature will have her way and this is the natural order of things by age.

Even after they have made the sexual change, it will be a factor in relationships. If it is not apparent in the beginning, it will not be as big a factor. More often than not, the individual will still find problems with acceptance. Hence, often moving to, and living in certain areas of a community where the lifestyle is accepted readily. The better Sun signs to have as friends under these circumstances are, Sagittarius, the air signs of Libra, Gemini and Aquarius, and sometimes Capricorn, perhaps even a Pisces.

In the end, the person who will have considered making this change, or who has made the change, will settle into a lifestyle that allows freedom of the mind.

The Point of Self is found, by starting on the first house cusp which represents the personal and physical being, then going through the chart allowing two years and four months for each house.

Doing so, you will find that the Point of Self is zero on the first house cusp, and seven years of age on the cusp of the fourth house. Age twenty-eight on the first house cusp after the first transit through the chart, results in new beginnings, and the next phase of life to begin.

My knowledge in this matter is limited, however, I've found that the charts I have do give some indication of the fifth house, and the twelfth house being involved. The more interesting feature is the presence of the moon in the twelfth house. The moon, representing womanhood and found in the house of restriction, and that of hospitalization. Pluto could be found in either the fifth house, seeking a change to a more enjoyable love life style, or in the sixth house in opposition to the house where their moon resides. Mars is often found in the fifth house as well.

EMOTIONAL CYCLES

There are many cycles involved in your life, and as you progress from day to day through you life. Among those cycles there is one more you may find of interest, the cycle of emotions. To the best of my knowledge the first studies done on these cycles, was performed by Professor Rex Hersey of the University of Pennsylvania.

These cycles are basically the same for men and women, with the exception that in the case of women, the emotional cycle may seem irregular at times because of their menstrual cycle, as it can cause interference. However, over a period of time each person will find they maintain a fixed sequence. It can vary on occasion by a few days, but for the most part it will remain constant.

The cycle's average five weeks from high to low, and the portion of these cycles that may interest the reader, is often the low portion. The reason for this interest is that this is often the part of the cycle that produces the most interest in lovemaking. It is believed that this is the stimulus needed to help bring some quiet times into your life, and to help you sleep.

You will find, perhaps to your liking or dislike, that your particular cycle does, or does not match that of your chosen mate.

You can track your highs and lows by using the chart offered here. Make a mark at the end of each day in the appropriate box as to your mood. This ranges from a +3 to a -3 in each square.

CHART OF EMOTIONAL CYCLES

Day		1	2	3	4	5	6
Elated	+3						
Happy	+2						
Pleasant feeling	+1						
Neutral	0						
Unpleasant feeling	-1						
Disgusted, or sad	-2						
Worried, or depressed	-3						

Day		7	8	9	10	11	12
Elated	+3						
Happy	+2						
Pleasant feeling	+1						
Neutral	0						
Unpleasant feeling	-1						
Disgusted, or sad	-2						
Worried, or depressed	-3						

Day		13	14	15	16	17	18
Elated	+3						
Happy	+2						
Pleasant feeling	+1						
Neutral	0						
Unpleasant feeling	-1						
Disgusted, or sad	-2						
Worried, or depressed	-3						

Day		19	20	21	22	23	24
Elated	+3						
Happy	+2						
Pleasant feeling	+1						
Neutral	0						
Unpleasant feeling	-1						
Disgusted, or sad	-2						
Worried, or depressed	-3						

Day		25	26	27	28	29	30
Elated	+3						
Happy	+2						
Pleasant feeling	+1						
Neutral	0						
Unpleasant feeling	-1						
Disgusted, or sad	-2						
Worried, or depressed	-3						

Day		31					
Elated	+3						
Happy	+2						
Pleasant feeling	+1						
Neutral	0						
Unpleasant feeling	-1						
Disgusted, or sad	-2						
Worried, or depressed	-3						

You must be honest with yourself when marking this chart, do not mark it higher or lower than you feel at the time. To get the accurate picture of your high and low parts, you must mark it correctly. Once you have this information, you can plan activities that require any part of your mood swings.

NIGHT OR DAY PERSON

If you check your temperature every hour from the time you get up in the morning, until you retire at night, you will find it raises or lowers. If it raises, you are a night person, if it lowers, you are a morning person. If you are aware of this fact, you will find that you will be the most efficient during the period of your high temperatures.

ASTROLOGICAL SYMBOLS

♈	ARIES	♂	MARS
♉	TAURUS	♀	VENUS
♊	GEMINI	☿	MERCURY
♋	CANCER	☽	MOON
♌	LEO	☉	SUN
♍	VIRGO	☿	MERCURY
♎	LIBRA	♀	VENUS
♏	SCORPIO	♇	PLUTO
♐	SAGITTARIUS	♃	JUPITER
♑	CAPRICORN	♄	SATURN
♒	AQUARIUS	♅	URANUS
♓	PISCES	♆	NEPTUNE

GLOSSARY

Ascendant
The ascendant (ASC.) is the sign found on the first house cusp.

Aspects used in this book.
Aspects have an orb of influence, and each is assigned so many degrees out of a 360 degree circle. In this book, the smallest amount of orb will be used to eliminate confusion.

A conjunction finds each planet within 8 degrees of each other's position, and within this orb of influence.

A sextile is planets 60 degrees apart, and the planets are within 7 degrees of this orb of influence.

A semi-sextile is 30 degrees apart, and the planets are unusually within 4 degrees of this orb of influence.

A trine is 120 degrees apart, and the planets are usually within 8 degrees of this orb of influence.

An opposition is 180 degrees, and the planets are usually within 8 degrees of this orb of influence.

A square is 90 degrees apart, and the planets are usually within 8 degrees of this orb of influence.

Chart or horoscope
Both words mean the same thing, and they refer to a map of the heavens at the time of a persons birth, or the beginning of some event.

Constellations.
Constellations used as reference in this book, are those associated with the Sun signs used in astrology, and are listed here.

Aries Occurs between - March 21st & April 19th
Taurus Occurs between - April 20th & May 20th
Gemini Occurs between - May 21st & June 20th
Cancer Occurs between - June 21st & July 22nd
Leo Occurs between - July 23rd & August 22nd
Virgo Occurs between - August 23rd & Sept 22nd
Libra Occurs between - Sept 23rd & October 22nd
Scorpio Occurs between - Oct 23rd & Nov 21st
Sagittarius Occurs between - Nov 22nd & Dec 21st
Capricorn Occurs between - Dec 22nd & Jan 19th
Aquarius Occurs between - Jan 20th & Feb 18th
Pisces Occurs between - Feb 19th & March 20th

Cusp
The cusp, is the beginning edge of each house division.

Elements
Each sign of the zodiac is associated with a particular element on earth.

> Aries, Leo and Sagittarius are the fire signs
> Taurus, Virgo and Capricorn are the earth signs
> Gemini, Libra and Aquarius are the air signs
> Cancer, Scorpio and Pisces are the water signs

Ephemeris
An ephemeris is a catalog of planetary positions in the heavens at any given time.

Houses
These are divisions of a 360 degree circle, each house receiving 30 degrees. In reality, in some cases the houses may have more, or less than 30 degrees when the horoscope is completed.

Luminaries
This refers to the Sun and the Moon.

Point of self - *PS*
The point of self, is where someone resides by age in their horoscope at any point in life. This is found by adding two years and four months to each house cusp starting with the first house cusp as the birth, and zero years.

Quarter composites
The horoscope is divided into quarters of three houses each, starting with the first house.

Stelliums
Normally a stellium consists of at least five planets in the same sign for the greater strength, However a combination of even three planets in a sign will have a some impact on life.

Reference materials.

'Marriage, Divorce & Astrology,'
Teri king
ISBN 0-85031-465-8 PUB. 1982

'How to Handle your Human Relations'
Lois Haines Sargent
American Federation of Astrologers - publisher

'Cycles'
Edward R. Dewey
Library of Congress Card Catalog number
70-130730

ISBN 1-882896-04-1
EAN 978-1-882896-04-2

www.ingramcontent.com/pod-product-compliance
Lightning Source LLC
Chambersburg PA
CBHW071305110426
42743CB00042B/1185